The Books of Elizabeth Bowen

Novels

Eva Trout (1968)
The Little Girls (1964)
A World of Love (1955)
The Last September (1929, 1952)
The Heat of the Day (1949)
The Death of the Heart (1939)
The House in Paris (1936)
To the North (1933)

Short Stories

Early Stories (1951)
Ivy Gripped the Steps (1946)
Look at All Those Roses (1941)

Non-Fiction

Seven Winters and Afterthoughts (1962)
A Time in Rome (1960)
The Shelbourne Hotel (1951)
Collected Impressions (1950)
Bowen's Court (1942, 1964)

Juvenile

The Good Tiger (1965)

These are Borzoi Books,
published in New York by Alfred A. Knopf

Pictures and Conversations

PICTURES AND CONVERSATIONS

by Elizabeth Bowen

WITH A FOREWORD BY

SPENCER CURTIS BROWN

NEW YORK: ALFRED·A·KNOPF

1975

ꞱZOI BOOK

D A. KNOPF, INC.

Grateful acknowledgment is made to Lord David Cecil, Cyril Connolly, John Bayley and Howard Moss for permission to quote from their articles or letters, and to George Weidenfeld and Nicolson Limited and Simon & Schuster, Inc. for permission to reprint the article on Bergotte from *Marcel Proust* edited by Peter Quennell, 1971.

Library of Congress Cataloging in Publication Data
Bowen, Elizabeth, (date). Pictures and conversations.
I. Title.
PR6003.06757P5   1974   823'.9'12 [B]   74-7753
ISBN 0-394-47896-7

Manufactured in the United States of America

Published January 7, 1975
Second Printing, March 1975

CONTENTS

FOREWORD

I

SOME TIME in the mid-nineteen-fifties, ELIZABETH
BOWEN asked me to be her literary executor.
Though touched and made proud by her confidence,
I did not, and this may seem an unforgivable, but
was certainly not a heartless, lack of forethought,
take any steps concerning this responsibility. Indeed, there may have been little I could have done.
Elizabeth was an entertaining but infrequent letter-
writer; nor did she keep, unless they were directly
concerned with her books, any letters she received
(not, at least, those which interested her and
which she at once answered; uninteresting ones,
which she knew that she should, but equally knew
that she never would, answer, were stacked in card-
board boxes all over the house). But one instruc-
tion she did specifically give me.

When she asked me to stay with her, early in
1972, she had shown me the draft of the first two
chapters of her book *Pictures and Conversations,*
and we talked a little of what might come in the
succeeding chapters she had outlined. The title,

taken from *Alice in Wonderland,* was significant, for the book would never have dealt with her own adult life, but only with images that her eyes had seen and with memories of things said to her. Then in July of that year, when I saw her in hospital, she had just learnt that she had not more than a year to live, and she told me that what she wanted most was to finish both this book and a short novel before she died. But the cancer weakened her more than she knew. She made some of the changes we had discussed in the second chapter and added a few exploratory paragraphs for a third, but could do no more. The day before she died she sent for me, and as there were others much closer to her than I, I knew she must have some message she wanted to give. The nurse had told me that she was very weak, under strong pain-killing drugs, and might not recognise me, but she did. She could hardly speak, but when I asked her "Do you want the fragment of the autobiography published," she suddenly gained strength and said clearly and firmly, "I want it published," and then she repeated it, "I want it published." So here it is. I do not think she ever regained consciousness, and died, quite painlessly, next day.

ELIZABETH LEFT very little unpublished work. She did not start books and go back to them; she either finished or rejected them. Nor had she, for several years, written any short stories. The second piece in this collection is therefore the beginning of the short novel she so wished to complete, which contains much of what is most characteristic of her writing—the immediate creation of suspense, the humour, the conciseness, the precision of description, whether of characters or place, the imposition of mood. She gave me, under her will, the power to have any unfinished novel completed by another hand of my choosing. What an impertinence that would be and how obviously impossible.

Thirdly, I have included a long article she wrote on Proust's character Bergotte. This article, though published in an expensively illustrated symposium edited by Peter Quennell (at whose request it was written), has never appeared before among her own works.

Next I have included a Nativity play she was asked to write for choral performances in Limerick Cathedral. It has been suggested to me by those I respect that this should not be included because it is so different from the work expected from Elizabeth Bowen. That seems to me a most excellent reason for including it. Herself a many-faceted person, her gifts were many-faceted too, and the play is certainly immensely skilful technically. But the most important reason for inclusion is that she was fond of it, and I think she would have liked to know it was in print.

Finally I have reprinted her "Notes on Writing a Novel" because she refers to them in her autobiographical chapters and because, though jotted down almost in telegraphic form, they indicate so much better than anyone else can some of the guide-lines she followed in her own writing. But no "rules" can convey genius. Once David Cecil, writing to her about *Eva Trout,* enumerated some of her gifts and then added "But the result is more than a combination of these qualities. A young producer once gave detailed instructions to the mature Ellen Terry about her performance. She said, 'I will do all the things you say—but after that I will do that little bit extra for which I am paid my salary.' You have that little extra bit." Few would disagree with him. And it has seemed a satisfying fortuity that, apart from their inherent interest, these four posthumously collected pieces, one of descriptive non-fiction, one of fiction, one of critical analysis and one written for public performance, should together illustrate in miniature something of the great variety of her gifts.

II

TWO OF Elizabeth's friends, both critics but with very differing backgrounds, wrote accounts of Elizabeth after her death; the first is of her generation, half English, half Irish, a friend ever since Oxford days; the second is younger, American, a poet knowing her only in her later years. Here are passages from each.

Cyril Connolly wrote, in the *Sunday Times* of London:

> She was an only child and in 1930 inherited the family home, Bowen's Court, a severely classical house from the golden age of the Anglo-Irish, about which she wrote a delightful book which is a compendium of family history.
>
> In the epilogue, written after the house had been sold and demolished, she sums up the role of the Anglo-Irish gentry.

> "My family got their position and drew their power from a situation that shows an inherent wrong. In the grip of that situation England and Ireland each turned to each other a closed, harsh, distorted face— a face that in each case their lovers would hardly know. . . . What runs on most through a family living in one place is a continuous, semi-physical dream. Above this dream level successive lives show their tips, their little conscious formations of will and thought. With the end of each generation the lives that submerged here were absorbed again. With each death, the air of the place had thickened; it had been added to. . . . Inside this frame, I have written about the Bowens out of what I do know but do not know why I know. Intuitions that I cannot challenge have moved me to colour their outlines in."

So much of her is in these brief quotations: her realism, her imagination, her consciousness of who she was and why she was—the end product of what she called "fairly ordinary Anglo-Irish gentry," whose main virtue was their independence and whom she defended with the spirited loyalty with which she defended all her friends, her way of life, the world of the heart and the intellect.

Her novels are often extremely funny, as in the opening of *Eva Trout,* and sometimes over-allusive in the Jamesian manner. She was at heart a romantic, with a keen sense of betrayal, the betrayal of youthful ideals, intellectual promise, worldly ambition. . . .

Her style is a writer's delight, there is an enjoyment of the grotesque, of absurd conversations as between Dublin ladies straight out of Congreve, a passionate sense of place, of love affairs, the interior decoration of not so humble homes, flashes of observation as of the Anglo-Irish lady tapping the turf fire with her brocaded evening slipper. She was the intellectual peer of her friends Virginia Woolf and Edith Sitwell, a poet content to work her imagination into the texture of her prose.

She belongs to the mainstream of English comedy inheriting from both Emily Brontë and Jane Austen but deeply influenced by Flaubert and Proust. Romantic despair was tempered by her natural gaiety and Christian good sense.

In the New York *Times* Book Review, Howard Moss wrote:

She was rare. A large-boned beauty with a face of such distinction that the only comparable one in recent history is Virginia Woolf's. It would be hard to imagine anyone kinder. But kindness, these days, suggests some sort of namby-pamby person, soft and easily swayed. Nothing could be farther from the truth. She could be acerbic, was one of the wits of her time, and could detect, from a great distance, the faintest whiff of the false. With the pretentious, she could be devastating.

The combination of a wit so accurate and a warmth so pervasive led to mistaken impressions. It was hard to believe that these usually incompatible forces were held in such arresting suspension. She was incapable of dishonesty. She was more generous than can be imagined and had no sense of the "strategy" of literary careers or the dark scrimmage of "reputations." She had so much intrinsic power that I don't think the idea of acquiring any ever crossed her mind. In all, the matter of semblances never came up, so strikingly positive was her impression, so absolutely steady the aura around her, and so precise what she thought and what she had to say.

She was intensely private but enormously enjoyed sociability. In fact, many of her qualities would have been paradoxical in a lesser person, and what was original in her work stems from that very doubleness: a true understanding of the most subtle undertows in human relationships and an absolute sense of social comedy. Not side by side but simultaneously. She gave every leverage to the individual, to friends, to anyone she loved, and she was a great friend of the young, which many famous writers are not. She was tough on bores by ignoring them, disliked diamonds in the rough and was the least snobbish person I knew.

But all of this is mainly anecdotal and nostalgic. The real thing, the important thing is the work. Just how important remains to be seen. There will be a reassessment, naturally. It's high time. Meanwhile, in regard to the mastery of English prose, I offer as evidence the end of this last paragraph of the introduction to *Ivy Gripped the Steps,* a book of short stories, all of which take place during the London blitz.

"This discontinuous writing, nominally 'inventive,' is the only diary I have kept. Transformed into images in the stories, there *may* be important psychological facts: if so, I did not realize their importance. Walking in the darkness of the nights of six years (darkness which transformed a capital city into a network of inscrutable canyons), one developed new bare alert senses, with their own savage warnings and notations. And by day one was always making one's own new maps of a landscape always convulsed by some new change. Through it all, one probably picked up more than can be answered for. I cannot answer for much that is in these stories, except to say that I know they are all true—true to the general life that was in me at the time. Taken singly, they are disjected snapshots—snapshots taken from close up, too close up, in the middle of the mêlée of a battle. You cannot *render,* you can only embrace—if it means embracing to suffocation point—something vast that is happening right on top of you. Painters have painted, and photographers who were artists have photographed, the tottering lacelike architecture of ruins, dark mass movements of people, and the untimely brilliance of flaming skies. I cannot paint or photograph like this—I have isolated; I have made for the particular, spot-lighting faces or cutting out gestures that are not even the faces or gestures of great sufferers. This is how I am, how I feel, whether in war or peace time; and only as I am and feel can I write. As I said at the start, though I criticise these stories now, afterwards, intellectually, I cannot criticise their content. They are the particular. But through the particular, in wartime, I felt the high-voltage current of the general pass."

These passages by her friends convey much, and brilliantly. My own notes are not extensions of, but additions to, them.

ELIZABETH WAS a writer but did not move in the world of writing. Many of her most enduring friendships were with authors—T. S. Eliot, Maurice Bowra, David Cecil, Isaiah Berlin, Connolly himself—but though she may have enjoyed and admired their writings, as they often, but not always, enjoyed and admired hers (neither Connolly nor Berlin, I think, read many of her novels), she chose her friends only for their intelligence or wit or sympathy or simple goodness. Uninterested in any talk of transient literary—still less critical—fashions she would not have given any impression to strangers meeting her casually that she was an author, far less so outstanding a one. Even to her close friends, she never (with very few exceptions) talked of books on which she was working, and never, herself, proffered talk of past books, her beautiful manners enabling her to appear to answer while actually diverting the talk. Indeed when one was in her company the subject of herself or her own life, past or present, did not arise. This was not from secretiveness but because she had no time for introspection; her eyes were always outward, observing other people. It was perhaps because she drew so much of her enjoyment and mental stimulus from observing others and sharing and extending their thoughts that she tended to keep her friends in compartments. She liked meeting the friends of her friends because there the mood was likely to be homogeneous, but she so arranged her life as not to be presented with and not to enter into differing attitudes of mind simultaneously. This was not because she wore a different mask to different people but because, so many-faceted, she could present to different people a different facet of the same personality. Those who knew her best realised, I think, that they did not, could not, see all of her—and that to very few could she show all, for there was never enough time. That question of time is perhaps indicative. She was so full of ideas herself, so creative of ideas in others, such fun to be with, that I doubt whether people ever felt that they had seen quite enough of her, however long the visit, however often she stayed with them or they with her. Never boring herself, she had a great gift for the graceful break if she ever felt that boredom or even satiety might impinge on her.

She was an immensely hard worker. While writing a book, she would seldom appear before the pre-lunch drink, and then retire again after lunch till five o'clock or so. When working, she read only for entertainment—countless detective stories, countless re-readings of Wodehouse, many American novels. Crosswords she detested, and of newspapers read only the lightest. But after five o'clock she longed for relaxation. She loved to be driven around country roads, stopping at small pubs. She loved meeting people and was happy to listen to trivia. She loved chatting over drinks. She loved and created gaiety of mind. She could be wise, but absolutely never pompous. And her boundless curiosity about people and places made her appear—and it was a genuine not an applied appearance—to be interested in a great variety of people and to be able to bring out what was most entertaining, most intelligent and most kind in them. Her impatience—it was great—was a social as well as a writer's asset for, easily bored herself, (she refrained from seeing again or politely withdrew from the long-winded) she condensed any thought into the fewest possible words, and her wit as a result was sharp, surprising, unpadded, precise. It was never malicious or destructive wit, but illuminating and full of her own enjoyment of the subject, an enjoyment she conveyed so that any gathering was lightened by her coming.

Utterly unsnobbish, as Moss remarked, either as regards class or simplicity of mind, she was aware of goodness in others as a positive quality and responded to it. She was a very frequent church-goer, and although in Ireland this may have coincided with a desire to "show the flag" of the Protestant Ascendancy, in England it arose from genuine Christian faith. The formalism of the Church appealed to her, as all formalism did, and to attend a service wherever she might be and to know and support the incumbent were for her a natural part of life. But she was unswayed by any attitudes—or lack of attitudes—towards religion in others. She was in fact unswayed by others in any sense, being strong and aware of herself emotionally and mentally. While she was in no way arrogant, it did not occur to her to pretend to herself or to others to underrate herself. That is perhaps why, though confident of (though never wholly satisfied with) the quality of her own writings, she was uninterested in acclaim, though extremely interested in having been able to communicate to readers, and she did keep many of the letters friends wrote to her after reading her books.

She thought an author's obligation, to herself and to others, was to write. She saw this obligation in proportion to duties imposed from outside whether by individuals or events, but the fulfilling of such outside duties did not, in her opinion, exempt her from her obligations to writing. Her answers in a radio interview, spontaneous and unconsidered as they were, illustrate this attitude.

INTERVIEWER: "Are you concerned by what happens in the world around you?"
ELIZABETH BOWEN: "I am less so than a number of people. I entirely believe the writers I have known who have said they've been reduced to absolute silence by the state of the world—not through lack of faith in their own powers but by some feeling that what they

are creating is futile, and why go on? It hasn't affected me like that at all, for better or worse. Just as in an air-raid, if you were a warden, which I was, you stump up and down the streets making a clatter with the boots you are wearing, knowing you can't prevent a bomb falling, but thinking, 'At any rate, I am taking part in this; I may be doing some good.' And just as, apart from the work I did during the war in propaganda for the Government, I went on writing and writing away—not, I think, altogether wrongly, but feeling, 'Well, this is the one thing I can do and what's the point in stopping it? If it's any good at any time, it's some good now.' "

Trying to picture her, it is her most beautifully shaped head and forehead which I first see. Her features were strong, yet completely feminine; she liked on occasion to dress superbly and to know that she had done so. Not vain, she knew that she had "presence." Knowing her strength, she also knew always that she was a woman, and that she attracted by so being.

OF HER EARLY CHILDHOOD in Dublin she has written in *Seven Winters*. The chapters printed here tell of the influence on her girlhood of her Anglo-Irish background and of the generations who had lived for three hundred years on the same land and for two hundred years in the same house. But this background, when she came to write her early books, she wished, if not to ignore, at least to put aside in her search for the outer world, for the new and the different. After leaving school and after realising that she had no satisfying gift as a painter, she had spent a year with one of her aunts in Italy. Then she came back to London to write—short stories only, for it was only of stories that she then conceived herself capable; but of that capability she was certain. And she had determination. The death of her mother (a loss so devastating that to the end of her life she would not willingly refer to it) and her father's long illness had necessitated that she must find her strength within herself. She found it and never lost it.

In 1923, soon after her return to London and after a very quick courtship, she married Alan Cameron, and it was a marriage which was to give much to each, for she and Alan in many ways complemented each other. He, who had had a long hard war as a Major in France and whose mind often went back not to the horrors but to the experiences of those times, was a first-class administrator. He had become, when they married, Director of Education for Northamptonshire, and it was there that they first lived. Soon he was given the more exciting and responsible post of Oxfordshire and they lived at Old Headington, at that time still outside though abutting Oxford. A few years later, Alan was selected for one of the most influential educational jobs in England, organising School and Adult Educational Programmes for the B.B.C., and they moved to London.

Because Alan had an ability and a position which was recognised in his own field, just as Elizabeth was recognised in hers, the marriage had a balance which I think was valuable to both, and his common sense, strength and unfailing kindness were certainly a support to her. And he not only enormously admired but enjoyed her writing. They had, too, a shared enjoyment of the same sources of laughter, and throughout there was a strong mutual devotion. It was not only a firmly founded but a happy marriage.

BUT IT HAD BEEN at Old Headington that Elizabeth came to know that group centred on the University who were to remain her friends for life and who responded to her quick but logical brain, to her ability to comprehend at once the basic point of an argument and to separate the incidental from the important, yet always to express herself with humour and lightness. With Elizabeth the individual and the writer were, I think to a rare extent, indistinguishable, and anyone reading the books, if they read both the fiction and the non-fiction, could perhaps for themselves assess the sort of person she must have been. It was at this period that the woman she was to become, and the writer she was to become, first took firm shape.

III

NEARLY EVERYTHING I say in this section on her writing is based on talks with her. What little is guesswork is obviously so. It is in no way the appraisal of a critic, but only the uninstructed thoughts of a friend in whose appreciation and understanding of her books she herself appeared to have confidence.

Because Elizabeth as a writer gradually changed in what she knew she had power to do and in what she wished to do, it is possible to trace something of those changes in her full-length writings. There were no such changes in the short stories, and Elizabeth herself, in the preface to the selection she made of her own stories *A Day in the Dark,* wrote:

As I see it, a writer of short stories is at his or her best sometimes, and sometimes not; and this is true equally at any age or in any year at which he or she happens to be writing. "Development" may appear in any one writer's successful novels; in successful stories, I hold it to be a myth. The short story is a matter of vision rather than of feeling. Feeling (which is important in the novel) does, or should, mature as one grows older. Of vision, one asks only that it should not lose its intensity—and I would say that if vision is there at all, that wish is usually granted.

Elizabeth's writing has a sharp divide. Of the first period, *A World of Love* is the climax. All her books certainly had one common quality—that no one else could possibly have been thought to have written any of them, for she had extreme individuality not only of style but of mind. And in all of them there is the humour, so taut, so beautifully timed, more widely based than Jane Austen's, even more economical in expression, but as feminine in a way to delight men as much as women. Aseptic, it was never malicious (there was nothing of "cattiness" in Elizabeth, whether as a person or as a writer). While delighting us, it also illuminated character and told us more about character, for Elizabeth would never pander to a reader merely to amuse; every word had to be for the purpose of the book. But having written her early stories solely, as she tells, from observation through which she herself could guess at characters, she soon progressed to moulding the observed not only to convey character to the reader but precisely to pin-point it. Neither she nor the reader any longer had to guess: she knew, for she had created; and the reader knew because she portrayed with an absolutely clear outline and selected exactly those details which would give a full and unmistakable character.

Other qualities in turn became more marked, but she never forgot a skill acquired. It was as if a musical conductor, having obtained the performance he wanted from one instrumentalist, then turned to another while keeping the orchestra playing, until all in turn could blend into the total interpretation he wanted from them. Perhaps one of the most noticeable of her qualities was the conciseness with which she wrote. Every book seemed to the reader to be much longer than it actually was. She wrote in draft very many more words than appeared in the novel, purposely withdrawing what she, as author, had to find out by having written but what she then realised she did not have to convey in words. "The test of what is to be written," she wrote in an essay on "Exclusion," "is . . . not least its power to make known, by suggestion or evocation of something further, what needs to be known without being told." She was a master of such evocation and she achieved it not merely by choice of words but even more by the use of rhythm in her sentences and paragraphs. No one could, without loss, skip or skim her writing. She wrote unintendingly but naturally for those for whom reading was, like writing, a creative act.

Then there is the element of time. All her novels, except *The Last September,* were set in the present, but the present was not last year or next year; it was the actual moment in which she was writing. This gives each detail in her book, whether a description of clothes, of conversation or of mood, a precisely true setting. The result is that, so far from seeming out-of-date, they seem of *all* time, because each is true to one time. So might an eighteenth-century "conversation" picture seem of all time, whatever the dress, whatever the background. On this point of exactness in time John Bayley, who with his wife, Iris Murdoch, had become very devoted to Elizabeth, wrote to her about her last novel:

> What I find especially stimulating and devastating about Eva and her whole ambience is the *modernity*. The sense of burning one's fingers with the present moment, which so many novels now try—with what fatiguing laboriousness—to give one, is yours from page one. Your "intouchness" is indeed marvellous.

In all her books, too, she was able—as, in a different medium, is a great painter—so to present a familiar object as to make the reader feel that he was now seeing it for the first time. This was perhaps due to the blending in her of both impatience and precision; of her desire not to waste words on what need not be described because it was obvious, together with her skill in selecting exactly what and only what, for that one moment and that one mood, was individual. The same gift enabled her to describe an apparently trivial action and yet show that underlying it was an urgency and, for the characters, a split second of dramatic awareness.

Next there is in all her novels, but increasingly, the feeling that under the light comedy of the assured social world of which she wrote, there are for her characters—whether consciously known or unconsciously felt—earth-tremors, so that the actual earthquake may at any time shatter their lives. In the preface to her collection of short stories *A Day in the Dark,* she wrote: "A number of my stories . . . have a supernatural element in them. I do not make use of the supernatural as a get-out; it is inseparable (whether or not it comes to the surface) from my sense of life. That I feel it unethical —for some reason?—to allow the supernatural into a novel may be one of my handicaps as a sincere novelist." She adhered to this ethic, but no one could have written her books who had not this feeling—however kept in bonds by the novelist—of the supernatural, and no one can read her books without being aware of it. It is one of the qualities which helped to create suspense and tension in the mind of the reader even though it was never used for purposes of suspense or tension in the actual plot. Connolly described her as "a romantic, with a keen sense of betrayal, the betrayal of youthful ideals, intellectual promise," etc. But she was certainly not a romantic in the sense either of avoidance of truth or of over-gilding the blessings in truth. Rather, what she saw was an Eden in the seconds after the apple had been eaten, when Evil was known, immanent and unavoidable but while there was still awareness of what Innocence had been. Her ability at the same time to create high social comedy and to make one believe that the Serpent was lying in wait, first obvious in *Friends and Relations* but increasingly so in *The House in Paris,* became intensified later, and though the comedy was always present, the sense of possible disaster became more acute.

Lastly, there is an increasing element of poetry in her writings. In a lecture once given in America on the poetic element in fiction (I have no text, merely a shorthand writer's attempt—perhaps inaccurate—to take it down), she said:

"We who tell the story find ourselves fighting against the apparent restrictions of prose language. . . . The frontier line between prose with its precision, and poetry with its infusion of what cannot be precise—that line, as I feel it, is beginning to yield, beginning to fade. We who tell stories are making our demands on the imagery of the poetic language; we are trying to fuse our words not only in their meanings but, as Shelley said they can be fused, also in their sounds. Our idea of style must have muscularity and strength, but it should also be capable of being luminous and transparent. We need to be subject to that force, that poetry of which Shelley says: 'It compels us to feel what we perceive and to imagine that which we know.' "

Elizabeth's mastery of all these varying elements, everything she had learned by writing, by constant experiment, by perpetual reaching forward, came to its climax in *A World of Love,* for that book, possessing all the pin-pointing of scenes and characters, the comedy, the underlying suspense which she had already perfected, was, in fact, a lyrical poem. Few who have read it can have failed for a while to feel that uprushing transport which only the sudden encounter with great art can give.

IN 1928, Elizabeth had written *The Last September,* a novel in no way autobiographical but set in that County Cork which had been her home and in a period, the nineteen-twenties of the Troubles, through which she had lived. Then in 1939 and during the first two years of the war, she wrote *Bowen's Court,* the history of the house in which she and her family before her had lived for so many generations. These two books became, much more in retrospect than at the time of writing, extremely important to Elizabeth. In a preface to a new edition of *The Last September,* published in *Seven Winters and Afterthoughts* in 1962, she wrote:

In real life, my girlhood summers in County Cork, in the house called Danielstown in the story, had been, though touched by romantic pleasure, mainly times of impatience, frivolity or lassitude. I asked myself *what* I should be, and when? In my personal memory, I did not idealise that September of 1920, the month in which this novel chose to be set. . . . When I sat in Old Headington, Oxford, writing *The Last September,* 1920 seemed a long time ago. By now (the year of writing, 1928), peace had settled on Ireland; trees were already branching inside the shells of large burned-out houses; lawns, once flitted over by pleasures, merged into grazing land. I myself was no longer a tennis girl but a writer; aimlessness was gone, like a morning mist. Civilisation (a word constantly on my lips in 1928) was now around me. I was in company with the articulate and the learned. Yet, onward from the start of *The Last September,* it was that other era that took command. . . . The action takes place during the "Troubled Times" —that is, the roving armed conflict between the Irish Republican Army and British Forces still garrisoning Ireland. Ambushes, arrests, captures and burnings, reprisals and counter-reprisals kept the country and the country people distraught and tense. . . . The position of such Anglo-Irish land-owning families as the Naylors, of Danielstown, was not only ambiguous but was more nearly heartbreaking than they cared to show. Inherited loyalty (or at least adherence) to Britain—where their sons were schooled, in whose wars their sons had for generations fought, and to which they owed their "Ascendancy," lands and power— pulled them one way; their own temperamental Irishness, the other. If it seems that Sir Richard and Lady Naylor are snobs with regard to the young English officers . . . their ambivalent attitude to the English, in general, should be noted; it is a marked Anglo-Irish trait.

Why was Lois, at her romantic age, not more harrowed or stirred by the national struggle around her? In part, would not this be self-defence? And world war had shadowed her school days: *that* was enough—now she wanted order. Trying enough it is to have to grow up, more so to grow up at a trying time. . . . Was it sorrow to her, Danielstown's burning? She was niece always, never child, of that house.

I *was* the child of the house from which Danielstown derives. Bowen's Court survived—nevertheless, so often in my mind's eye did I see it burning that the terrible last event in *The Last September* is more real than anything I have lived through.

Of the first germs of *Bowen's Court,* I have a very clear memory. I was staying with her there in the late nineteen-thirties, and anyone who stayed with her could not help but be aware, almost as physical presences (though not at all in the sense of "haunting") of the generations of Bowens who had made her, the house and the whole relationship of the house to its village of Kildorrery and to the other great houses of the County, generations of whom she, while seldom speaking unless perhaps to tell of the original of a portrait or how the house lacked one corner, was herself continuingly aware. One afternoon I said to her that she must one day write the history of the house—that she owed it to the house. And that it would be, besides, fascinating as a record of the close-knit society, English but in no way English, Irish but in no way Irish—the families of the vanishing Protestant "Ascendancy." She would not believe at first that anyone would be interested, but her American publishers, the Knopfs, who loved her as a friend as much as they loved her books, encouraged her and undertook to publish it whenever she wanted. She never ceased to be grateful to them. As a picture of that small but unique corner of history, it is, I think, of great value. But it is in the later chapters, dealing with her father's and her own life there, and especially in the foreword written for a new edition in 1964, that she shows so much of herself. In 1930, her father had died while she was in the house with him:

> I was the first woman heir; already I had changed my father's name for my husband's. We had no children.
>
> We continued, onwards from 1930, to live for the greater part of the time in England, where Alan Cameron worked and we had a home. . . . Not until 1952 was there any question (that was to say, any possibility) of our taking up a continuous life at Bowen's Court. Nonetheless, since the place had become mine it became familiar to me at every time of the year. . . . Existence there, though in fact it was discontinuous, did not seem so: each time one came back, it was as though one had not been away.

Elizabeth's mother, also Anglo-Irish, had been one of ten children, and there were countless cousins to whom Elizabeth remained very close throughout her life, and who with their families were frequent visitors to Bowen's Court. "It became part of the memories of many children." It became, indelibly, part of the memories of many friends, too, for Elizabeth and Bowen's Court seemed for many people to be a single entity, as a good rider seems one with his horse. And then came the ending:

> The house, having played its part, has come to an end. . . . The shallow hollow of land, under the mountains, on which Bowen's Court stood is again empty. Not one hewn stone left on another on the fresh-growing grass. Green covers all traces of the

foundations. Today, so far as eye can see, there might never have been a house there.

One cannot say that the space is empty. More, it is as it was—with no house there. How did this come to be?

It was not foreseen. Early in 1952, upon my husband's retirement from work, he and I left London to live at Bowen's Court. This was the life we had always promised ourselves. We brought back with us furniture which, originally Bowen's Court's, had been absent long—first in Dublin, afterwards in England: travelled tables and chairs were reunited with those which had never known anything but County Cork. The house, after its many stretches of patient emptiness, of returns only to be followed by departures, looked like, now, entering upon a new phase of habitation—full and continuous habitation, such as it had been built for. It made us welcome. This home-coming was like no holiday visit. In spite of the cold of a bitter January, all promised well. We had the Spring of that year, and the early summer. But then one night, that August, Alan Cameron died in his sleep.

I, remaining at Bowen's Court, tried to carry on the place, and the life which went with it there, alone. Already I could envisage no other home. I should, I thought, be able to maintain the place somehow. Had not others done so before me?

For a while this expectation of settled continuity in the place she loved continued. The peace for that while drove out distress. It was, after all, the first time she had lived in it as her own permanent house; her own permanent, as she thought, resting place. Buoyed up by being there, as by an elixir,

she was able, setting the scene in County Cork itself, to write *A World of Love.*

But gradually realities—financial realities—
closed in on her.

I had not enough money, and I had to face the
fact that there never would be enough. Anxiety, the
more deep for being repressed, increasingly slowed
down my power to write, and it was upon my earnings,
and those only, that Bowen's Court had by now come
to depend.

Fortunately there were outside events which
occupied her mind. She had been appointed, one of
two women, to serve on the Royal Commission on
Capital Punishment, and the work—involving not
only constant meetings and discussions and studies
of the MacNaghten rules and insanity laws but also
visiting most of the long-term prisons in England
and Scotland and many in America—continued for
over two years. It was hard work, but because she
knew the importance of it and because she enjoyed
working with people of trained intelligence, it did
keep her mind from her own worries and so was
helpful for her. And she had the knowledge at the
end that she had been of constructive help. In the
radio interview I quoted earlier, she was asked:

INTERVIEWER: "You said they wanted a second woman
and they wanted a writer on the Commission. In what
way do you feel you yourself, as both, contributed
most to the report?"

ELIZABETH BOWEN: "Every member of the Commission developed some personal line in their approach, and I myself brought in my particular point, which was that only physical provocation counts as provocation which can turn murder into manslaughter or make it just another homicide. And it may have been either as a writer and an imaginative person, or as a woman, that to me continuous mental torture is equally provocative. . . ."
INTERVIEWER: "Did you get your way in the report?"
ELIZABETH BOWEN: "We recommended the inclusion of verbal provocation."

During these years, too, she was given an Honorary Doctorate by Trinity College, Dublin, which especially pleased her for it had been her father's university, and later by Oxford. And she went frequently to America, giving courses in colleges in the Middle West, which she loved, and later at Princeton, and staying often with friends. For she loved America, the freshness of it, the vitality of it, and America in turn loved the freshness and vitality in her. But postponement could not help her.

Matters reached a crisis. By 1959 it had become inevitable that I should sell Bowen's Court.

The buyer was a County Cork man, a neighbour. He already was farming tracts of land, and had the means wherewith to develop mine, and horses to put in the stables. It cheered me also to think that his handsome children would soon be running about the rooms—for it was, I believe, his honest intention, when first he bought the place from me, to inhabit the house. But in the end he did not find that practicable, and who is to blame him? Finally, he decided that there was nothing for it but to demolish the house entirely. So that was done.

It was a clean end. Bowen's Court never lived to be a ruin.

Loss has not been entire. When I think of Bowen's Court, there it is. And when others who knew it think of it, there it is, also. . . . There is a sort of perpetuity about livingness, and it is part of the character of Bowen's Court to be, in its silent way, very much alive.

It was while she was undergoing the stress of knowing that to keep up the house might be impossible and that to part with it was unthinkable, that she decided to write her book on Rome. This was good therapy. It meant not only going to a completely different place, but immersing herself in two thousand years of the past, which she knew to be around her and of which she could, while there, first learn as a scholar might, from books, and then absorb as a writer might, through the senses and emotions. The result, *A Time in Rome,* was by any standard a tour de force. It conveyed in a single book the straightforward facts of the present city blended with the sensuous impact of it on sight, on taste, on touch, combined with the history of twenty centuries painted for us by a selection and illumination of significant detail—the Roman *domus,* Saint Paul brandishing his citizenship in the face of representatives of that State he came to challenge and to change, the society in which Cellini could live, Garibaldi's soldiers taunting the liberty-suppressing

French by blaring the *Marseillaise*. It is at once an irresistibly emotional and brilliantly intelligent book. She needed at this time to use her analytical brain on something outside her own imagination, on stones existing or known to have existed, on those who had lived in flesh and left their actions to speak for them. This use of her brain was both a pleasure and an excitement for her. But brain alone could not have provided the poetry or the artistry which made the book so completely satisfying a whole.

It was only shortly after *Rome* was completed that the final decision about Bowen's Court had to be and was made. Elizabeth—in New York, for she could not bear at such a time to be in Ireland—had a bad breakdown of health. She felt, I believe, guilt that she had failed her ancestry by failing to pass on her inheritance. She recovered. She returned to England and was too clear-headed ever to dwell on spilt milk. Thereafter, though living first, through the kindness of the Isaiah Berlins, in Headington, and later in the house she bought in Hythe, so full of memories of her mother, she still spent much time visiting America. Soon she wanted to write again, but her approach was to be different. Writing *Rome,* she had used her brain deliberately to occupy her attention while her emotional wounds were at their most painful. In that brain she had great resources, and she now chose as a novelist to use them to keep her life creatively and satisfyingly full. Because there were many aspects to her gifts, she could turn with excitement and interest and delight to the making use of another aspect and turning it to her own creative purposes. Hence the approach of her last two novels differs from that of those earlier. She came to write consciously and intentionally from maturity. Never again was she to write those short stories of which she said, "The short story is a matter of vision rather than of feeling." She deliberately sought new techniques and all the excitement of learning to express her own individual music on a new instrument. Never content merely to repeat, she wanted to and did constantly move forward into new areas, both of comprehension for herself and of communication to others. Courage was something she never lacked; she was—I use her word from the unfinished chapters—as "belligerent" towards idleness of mind in her work as towards despair in her life. There was new ground into which she could move, and she enjoyed both the effort and the success of the conquest. It was this moving forward which kept her always young, always unbeaten, and perhaps always as near content as was possible in her later post-Bowen's Court years.

This very desire to progress caused, or perhaps was caused by, a differing standpoint so that, still mirroring the same truth, she reflected it from a different angle. In her last two novels she no longer conveyed that there were earth-tremors beneath the feet of her characters; we knew that the earthquake had already come. She still showed certainly a world in which Innocence was remembered, but it was now a world in which the Serpent was already on the advance towards moments of triumph everywhere, over the society of man, the body and the mind—everywhere except over the invincibility of the spirit. That that last was invincible she never had, nor in her writing allowed, any doubt. "Chance is better than choice; it is more lordly. Chance is God, choice is man." And yet her sense of comedy—that unquenchable, incisive but never ironical comedy—irradiated the later books even more than the earlier. She remained always as fascinatingly amused and amusing in her books as in her talk or in her mind.

In *The Little Girls,* she for the first time deliberately tried, as she said when discussing with me the writing of it to present characters entirely from the outside. She determined never to tell the reader what her characters were thinking or feeling. She recalled that once when she had remarked to Evelyn Waugh that he never told his characters' thoughts, he had replied, "I do not think I have any idea what they are thinking; I merely see them and show them." In a way vastly different from Waugh's, she set herself the technical puzzle of writing a book "externally." She enjoyed doing it. That it was not easy and that the structure might not have been entirely successful in her own mind seemed evident to me from her uncharacteristic uncertainty while finishing it. She had completed the first draft while staying with me and had asked me to read it. I had made tentative and halting comments about the steps by which the reader was led to the ending, and she at once started to make the changes, and brought the new pages down each evening to discuss them. Although she had often asked for my suggestions, I had previously only referred to what I knew she herself intended but had, after her excisions, not perhaps made clear. I do not think she would, as in this case, have made a basic alteration—nor certainly would I have proposed one—had she herself been satisfied that she had expressed on paper a clear reflection of the image she had in mind. Somewhere I have the pages which she kept of the original ending, but I will never print them, for that was not her wish. Maybe some day a thesis-writer will compile a learned, but I hope not dull, comparison of the two versions.

Her next book, *Eva Trout,* was, however, a complete fulfilment. Here again she was aiming at a method of narration she had not previously attempted. Always before she had shown characters reacting to a situation. In *Eva,* she showed a character creating the situations herself. Elizabeth was relaxed while writing it, and confident that she had succeeded. Neglecting none of the skills she had worked out from her by now long experience of writing, drawing on the emotions accumulated by instinct, by sympathy and by wisdom, she created a book which gave her real satisfaction and gave to many a feeling that this was her most fascinating and effective, as *A World of Love* had been her most poetical, novel. Anyone who admires her work must be glad for her that this novel, which she did not of course know to be the last she would ever complete, was in many ways a culmination of all her skills, and that she was happy with and about it.

IV

OF HOW the unwritten chapters of the autobiographical book might have continued, I can speak only of Section IV. On the impetus which caused Elizabeth to start any one piece of writing, she was quite definite. It did not arise first from a conception of a character, or of a conflict, or of a continuing plot, least of all from any urge to express an emotion or illustrate a theory. It was sparked off always from the memory of something seen—a corner of a room, a view through a doorway, an effect of light on a garden. Such glimpses would not be consciously stored—she did not know she had remembered them. The glimpse was always of a sight slightly mysterious; the fully comprehended either remained with her permanently or was forgotten. But the mystery, the question unsolved by the eye and unknowingly secreted, would strongly, many years later, flash into her mind and she knew she wanted to write. I can give an odd example of this. One autumn evening when we were walking across cut cornfields the low full moon threw shadows right across the valley, and I foolishly kicked up my heels and made the shadows dance. Very many years later, in a quite different place and different mood, Elizabeth suddenly broke off to say, "Do you remember when you made those shadows dance?" It was not my action she remembered, but the slight eeriness and mystery of the mile-high jigging moon-shadows that had, from nowhere, flashed back on her. Such flash might not even appear in the book at all, but it was the flash which caused the urge to create.

The only other light I can shed is that after we had discussed the book and the outline, I wrote to her, and though the letter itself has no interest I quote it because she had kept it with her manuscript and her notes.

Thinking more about the book as a whole—relationship between the writer and the written, I hope you'll find it possible in later sections, as in the first, to keep the balance—i.e., relationship can't be shown unless writer is shown. Not, of course, "emotional life of," but the types of world in which you have, as adult, been cast either by own inclination or by necessity (husband's job and pleasures, etc.) or by results of own authorship (overlapping, but not entirely, with own inclinations). This *you* may find uninteresting but although what at any time you may have wanted to—had to—write may have risen from recalled place, yet the bricks used to build the story must arise from experiences and observations only obtainable from the lives you have led. And the "flashes" themselves would have been different if you'd spent your life with a pianist in sunny Naples. So some outline necessary of the differing moods created—at the time or in recollection—by differing periods of your life. (This too can lead to what is *not* secreted—i.e., the comprehended giving no spur to wonder.) And does the unwilled but apparently compulsive secreting and subsequent resurgence of the "flash" tie up with the witchcraft theme?

Perhaps she might have made some use of the letter; more probably not. We will never know now, and are the poorer for not knowing.

On February 22, 1973, she died. Though she had not lived in, nor had a house, far less a home, in Ireland for more than fourteen years, she wished to be buried in Kildorrery, in the church standing within the grounds of Bowen's Court itself. Only her relations and very close friends could go to the funeral there, but the church was full to overflowing and packed with flowers, for every villager came to show respect and bring gifts to this last Bowen. Elizabeth would have received them not with surprise but with happiness.

SPENCER CURTIS BROWN

Suffolk
September 1973

xlii

E· B·

Pictures and
Conversations

I

ORIGINS

T HE DAY this book was begun I went for a walk.
The part of Kent I am living in has wide views,
though also mysterious interstices. It can be considered to have two coastlines: a past, a present—
the former looks from below like a ridge of hills,
but in fact is the edge of an upland plateau: originally the sea reached to the foot of this. Afterwards,
the withdrawal of the sea laid bare salty stretches,
formerly its bed; two of the Cinque Ports, Hythe,
New Romney, consequently found themselves high-
and-dry, as did what was left of the Roman harbour
under the heights of Lympne. . . . The existing
coastline, a long shallow inward curve westward
from Folkestone to the far-out shingly projection
of Dungeness, is fortified for the greater part of its
way by a massive wall, lest the sea change its mind
again. Inside the sea-wall, the protected lands keep
an illusory look of marine emptiness—widening,
west of Hythe, into the spaces of Romney Marsh,
known for its sheep, its dykes, its sunsets and its

solitary churches. On a clear day, the whole of this area meets the eye: there are no secrets.

Not so uphill, inland. The plateau, exposed to gales on its Channel front, has a clement hinterland, undulating and wooded. It is cleft by valleys, down which streams make their way to the sea; and there are also hollows, creases and dips, which, sunk between open-airy pastures and cornfields, are not to be guessed at till you stumble upon them: then, they are enticing, breathless and lush, with their wandering dogpaths and choked thickets. Into a part of such a region, rather to the east, my Saturday morning walk took me—looking for a road I had known sixty years ago. There seemed no reason why it should no longer be there.

It was. Slanting upward from Seabrook, it zigzags across the face of a steep slope, finally to emerge from a tunnel of greenery, and terminate, at a high-up point where once stood Hythe's railway station. The ascent is continuous, but gentle.

On your left, as you mount from Seabrook, is the sea—ever farther below, out there beyond the Military Canal. Also below you, but mostly tree-hidden, runs the trafficky main thoroughfare, A 259. On your right, you are accompanied by the derelict cutting of what was a single-track railway line—first above you, then on the same level, then, as the road rises, risen above. Where it used to deepen, the cutting has silted up and become a jungle, overhung by vertical woods, invaded by saplings. Here

4

and there, buttresses of South Eastern & Chatham brickwork, darkened by moss and time, remind you that this primitive-looking landscape is in origin structural and was manmade. The road shows signs of being of the same epoch as the vanished railway, and of surviving only because *it* was impossible to remove. Each side, it is encroached upon by its grassy verges; remnants of some attempt to "surface" it adhere, in macerated tar-dark patches, to what elsewhere is gutted as though by tropical torrents, fins of rock bespeaking unthinkable cruelty to motor-cars. Accordingly, contrary to my fears, there has been not more than half-hearted residential development. Late-coming villas and bungalows peter out still not far from Seabrook; on the Channel side, for a little way farther up, costlier homes in the Spanish manner (patios, ironwork) cliffhang on slithery pine-clad slopes, but there are but few of them. Not a soul to be seen, or as much as heard; the road that morning was as unfrequented as when I frequented it first. Nothing of its character was gone. The May Saturday morning was transiently, slightly hysterically sunny, with a chill undertone.

When there had been nothing for some time, I came to—or was come upon, as one might be by an apparition—a garden created by someone in the fertile, leaf-mouldy bed of the cutting. No house was near it, only a shack in which to camp for a night. This less was a garden than a flowering

5

glade, glimmering and sensuous. Young "weeping" birches trailed veils of foliage golden rather than green; white rhododendrons were in bloom like white lamps in daylight; magnolias dropped upon their chalice buds. . . . Having ascended past this, the road made later, as ever, a sharp turn in order to cross a bridge.

The bridge's command of the line it was built to span enabled us—once, long ago, as children—to watch the train coming romping out of the distance, loudened by the acoustics of the gulley. . . . What had been the perspective was now blocked by the falling across it of a huge tree, whose deadness accentuated the hush. Weeds sprouting between its torn-up roots, brambles matting its shattered branches, the tree stayed wedged there: nobody's business. Among my pictures of here was a corpse of another kind: a sheep, come upon by me and another girl. Its body hideously torn open, bowels gushing forth, blood rusting its clotted wool, flies walking about on its open eyes, it lay as though nested in the deep, springy grass edging the road. We skirted it, sliding glances at it but saying nothing. I imagine that floundering downward, as sheep do, through the trees from a grazing patch on the skyline—there *were* sheep up there—into the trap of the cutting, it had been hit by a train, then been dragged by somebody up the embankment and cast away. The day after, in silent, dreadful accord, we went back to look: it was still there—but the next

6

gone, as though it had walked away. But that was far from the last of it. "I know where there's a wood with a dead sheep in it," Sheikie Beaker announces in *The Little Girls,* adding, "Some boys showed me." No boys showed us. No wood hid our sheep, it lay at the roadside. Also, Sheikie's sheep—though, from what she hints, some way into decomposition —was not mutilated; otherwise she'd have said so. Who, though, *was* my fellow-conspirator in that entire silence? (We never reported the sheep, being ashamed.) All my companions of that year are as clear as day to me, or at least as yesterday; her only I cannot identify, either by face or name. She is blotted out.

THERE WAS, or we held there to be, only one train. Indefatigably (if that were so) in motion, it shuttled to-fro over the short track between Sandling Junction and the terminal, Sandgate, its purpose being in some part military, for on top of the bluff over Sandgate station (which was in Seabrook) is Shorncliffe Camp. A poor day when soldiers were not aboard! Soon after passing under the bridge, on its way to Sandling, the train underwent a personality-transformation: woods began, giving it, as it tailed away into them to at last vanish, the flickering secretiveness of a reptile. . . . The road, once over the bridge, said goodbye to the railway and struck off on a course of its own.

Nothing was banal round here. Inland, the

7

steep overhanging scenery took on the look of a painted backdrop: one had the sensation of gazing up not so much at trees, rocks and bastions of evergreen as at depictions of them. Yet with this went a suggestion of Alpine danger. Here or there, creeper-dimmed gabled houses sat, as it were perilously, on brackets; while above tree-level was that bald skyline, on which (as said) were isolated some few sheep. And what was *behind* this canvas?—the rest of England.

For all that, it was the foreground I stood upon that possessed me. Underfoot, it lost nothing by being *terra firma:* actual and tangible, it remained magic. Able to be rambled about on, in, into, and, one might have thought, penetrated to the depths of their being, these scanty backwoods, road, bridge, cutting, eluded familiarity, keeping about them the magnetism of things, or scenes, on some other, aloof planet. . . . The road over the dropping-away sea smelled of sunshine and warmed lichen on rocks. Flowers erratically scattered their way along it: never was there a plethora of anything—a tuft or two of yellow flowering broom, and in turfy ditches scarlet-tipped lady's-fingers, rare harebells, and, later, the mauver blue of wild scabious. Vetches wove themselves into the longer grass.

I knew the place for less than a year, never in autumn: by the middle of that one summer we had gone. And seldom did I make my way up there by myself. Nobody stopped me; no danger attached in

8

those days, or was thought to, to the solitary, un-
restricted movement of little girls. But, it seems, I
safeguarded myself against any onset of what could
possibly disturbingly be poetic by being perpetually
(and, I must say, enjoyably) in company—that of
boon companions. So the road came to be fraught
with rowdy dramas of the kind children can and do
manufacture and would rather die than exist without; throughout which I registered what I loved
with such pangs of love (that is to say, registered
what was round me) only out of the corner of an
eye, only with an unwilling fraction of my being.
This was the beginning of a career of withstood
emotion. Sensation, I have never fought shy of or
done anything to restrain.

MY MOTHER AND I, that year, were living at Seabrook, that I might share a governess with the little
Salmons, daughters of the rector of Old Cheriton.
This still being in the nature of an experiment, our
existence was tentative, temporary, the villa we occupied having been taken furnished—our own belongings, lately brought over from Ireland, remained
behind at Lyminge, in another villa we had called
Erin Cottage. Seabrook, an early example of ribbon-
development, consisted, and still does, mainly of
smallish early-Edwardian dwellings strung out along
the Hythe-Folkestone road. There had been strate-
gic reasons for each of our many moves, in the last
few years, to and fro in the triangle formed by

Hythe, Folkestone and Lyminge. Seabrook stood for one of the intermissions from Lindum, my Folkestone day-school, where—while thinking as highly of the school as ever—my mother feared lest I suffer from overwork. That was the least of my troubles, for I was lazy, but such were her periodic dreads. "Overwork" had officially been the cause of my father's breakdown. My mother's family, the Colleys, had had misgivings as to her marriage to Henry Bowen, on the ground that the Bowens of Bowen's Court, County Cork, were rumoured to have an uncertain mental heredity. My paternal grandfather, Robert, had died in the throes of a violent mania brought on by a continuous quarrel with his heir (Henry); and there had been other cases of instability, due, it was understood, to first-cousin marriages back through the Bowen pedigree. To the Colleys, undeviatingly sane, ensconced, since their arrival in Ireland, in that central and civilised part of it known as The Pale, there could have seemed to be something fey and outlandish about those unpopulated stretches of County Cork with their unforgotten battlefields and abounding ruins. Also, Bowen's Court, architecturally solid enough, was the residence or at least the abiding headquarters of my father's large brood of brothers and sisters, who, whether or not Henry brought home a bride, would continue to see the mansion in that light: that is, they perceived no reason for moving out. Nor had my father very

10

much money, the enraged Robert having left all that he possibly could away from him. The house and lands could not, to the chagrin of Robert, be diverted from Henry, being entailed.

However, this being clearly a case of love, optimism prevailed: the marriage went through. I, born nine years later, was the one child of it. The young couple shelved the Bowen's Court problem by setting up house in Herbert Place, Dublin, he being a member of the Dublin Bar. All was happiness till the blow fell—his "breakdown," which was in fact the beginning of an agonising mental illness. Repressed forebodings now came again to the surface. Certified, by his own wish, he was sent for treatment to a mental hospital outside Dublin; my mother and I were ordered away by the doctors. Better for us to be across the sea, for even the idea of our nearness agitated him. She was told, also, that in going away, taking me with her, she was doing not only the best for him but the best for me. So we took off for England when I was seven. A heartbreaking decision for her to make: she must have been torn by the rights and wrongs of it. She showed me no signs, however, of what she was going through, and I asked no questions. Here we were, adventurers in this other country. Of her constant, underlying, watchful anxiety with regard to me, as my father's child, I have only had knowledge afterwards. Her advice "You must never tire your brain," the concern when I had a fever and

ran a temperature, together with the periodic re-
movings of me from Lindum, seemed to me little
more than a gentle fad, which occasionally had
pleasing outcomes—such as the extension of summer holidays. She would not have me taught to
read till I was seven (so that I should not burn
out my eyes, she said) and even after that used to
read aloud to me, a delight so great that it has
spoiled me for being "alone with a book." She
besought me not to get freckles on my hands—"All
Bowens get freckles on their hands.". . . I in no
way connected anything with my father's plight.

Otherwise she was altogether without fussi-
ness. I was let run wild, to an extent at which
other mothers lifted their eyebrows—falling off
horses, flopping about in the sea (made dangerous
for non-swimming children along these beaches, by
shelving shingle), plunging dementedly round and
round till I fell smack down on the roller-skating
rink, or death-diving on the precipitous Folkestone
switchback railway, when money was to be found.
I was a tough child, strong as a horse—or colt. I
had come out of the tensions and mystery of my
father's illness, the apprehensive silences or chaotic
shoutings (while he was still there with us in the
Dublin house) with nothing more disastrous than
a stammer. Not "nervous," I was demonstrative and
excitable: an extrovert.

Arriving in England, with our way to make
and our destiny uncertain, my mother and I were

not so alone as might be supposed. A grapevine of powerful Anglo-Irish relatives instantly took us into their keeping, passing us from hand to hand. We settled in south-east Kent (after a round of exploratory visits elsewhere) under the aegis of Cousin Isabel Chenevix Trench, widowed daughter-in-law of the late Archbishop of Dublin, who lived with her striking-looking growing-up family in Radnor Park, Folkestone, and Cousin Lilla Chichester, a childless dowager who commanded Sandgate from an ilex-dark eminence. (Enfield, her Victorian-Italianate home, reappears in one of my stories, "The Inherited Clock.") Without those two, our position—in those days, when everything was rather more right-and-tight—might have been ambiguous: it was not the thing for a woman other than a widow to be without a husband, and my mother was suspiciously lovely-looking, in addition to being accompanied by me. I learned not how the land lay but how it might have from a chance conversation, when I was about nine. "What is 'blackmail'?" I asked her, out of the blue. We were wandering about Hythe, near the canal. She thought, then said: "That would be, if somebody came to me and threatened to spread horrible stories about us unless I gave them money." "Oh," I said, knowing how little money we had. "But," she went on, not only with her usual serenity but with an air of distinct triumph over the putative situation, "that would not matter, because I should simply go to Cousin Isabel and Cousin Lilla, and they would tell everybody that those were lies." This impressed me, not in terms of respectability (which I don't imagine I'd ever heard of) but as proof of the dominance of my more or less synonymous race and family: the Anglo-Irish—with their manner of instantly striking root into the interstices of any society in which they happened to find themselves, and in their own way proceeding to rule the roost. One could perpetually be vouched for.

Which benefactress put us in touch with the Salmons, or initiated the plan of sharing the governess, I am not certain. We had had, already, one unofficial view of the Salmons when, out of a blend of spiritual and geographical curiosity, we had strayed from Hythe and attended mid-morning church at St. Martin's, Old Cheriton. It being a summery summer, a June Sunday, the two girls were wearing white muslin frocks, together with large floppy leghorn hats from beneath which fell cataracts of well-brushed hair, the elder's honey-yellow, the younger's dark. Story-book children. One was one size larger, one one size smaller, than I. Coming out, when the service was over, they smiled at us, newcomers to their father's flock— but we did not at that time expect to know them. Of their mother nothing was to be seen but a handsome back: she was animatedly talking to some parishioners. Mr. Salmon, from whom we had had an invigorating sermon, had features of an initial harshness lit up by originality and engaging charm: it was by resembling him that his little girls were redeemed from more ordinary childish prettiness. . . . My mother would have been as carried away as I was, had she not been in trouble with her conscience: my father, whose ethics continued to rule us, disapproved infidelity to one's parish church —we'd had no right to desert from St. Leonard's, Hythe. This was an escapade we must not repeat. The Salmons bade fair to remain an attractive memory.

Fate spun her wheel, and things turned out otherwise. Now, at a quarter-to-nine every weekday morning, I and the governess, Miss Clark, met at a corner in Seabrook, outside the Fountain Hotel— she coming from Sandgate, where her father was senior curate. She was an able young woman, trim in outline. In spite of a touch of the Gallic about her style—quick-moving, bright, rather prominent dark eyes, an alternately ruby and amethyst velvet ribbon threaded between the frizzy puffs of her hair —Miss Clark transpired to be more English than anyone I had yet met. Her manner was incisive. She could, I imagine, have gone far in any career—and perhaps did, subsequently? I disliked her only when she was sarcastic, or when she picked on me about my stammer, which in her view was due largely to faults of character: over-impatience, self-importance. "You try and get too much out at the same time," she would point out. "Concentrate on *one* thing, draw a deep breath, then say it *slowly.*" Together we went under the railway bridge (a lofty arch supporting the single line) and then on up Horn Street which, said to be pre-historic, shared the trough of a valley with the Seabrook brook, on its way to the sea. One ended by taking a short-cut up a steep field made marshy by many springs: when those overflowed then froze, as in the course of that winter they once or twice did, one had the extra sensation of ascending a glacier.

At the top stood the atmospheric rectory.

Contrary to my story-book notion of English parsonages, this one did not ramble and was not rose-clad. In shape it was like a domino on end. Behind (where was the hall-door) it looked into a wood in which was a rookery; but on *this* side three rows of sky-reflecting windows beamed on one as one squelched up the short-cut. Benevolently, the place looked haunted. In this house I remained with the Salmons throughout the day, Miss Clark dropping me back in Seabrook towards evening.

I felt a familiarity with the place from the first moment, and still do, and always shall—though it is no more. Between then and now it went through varying fortunes, not always clerical: it became, for instance, the residence, at one time, of one of the baroque relatives of my friend Tony Butts. Ultimately left empty, camped in now and then by a passing tramp, it caught fire and was burned to the ground. The wood behind it was felled. Yet, gone, it is not as though it had never been. The front rooms had in their nature—for all their ample windows and wide outlook—an inherent duskiness, comfortable and congenial; those at the back were intriguingly gloomy at any hour. At the back was situated "the parish room," with its resonant bare floor, hard chairs, upright piano. Two staircases, many-doored landings, blind closets, cavernous cellars, attics and, above all, weirdly misleading echoes made this house ideal for hide-and-seek—best of all in the dark, in the short days: winter. Rushing about was the nearest to violence we ever came.

Whether or not for that reason, I hit it off better with the rectory than I did with its tantalising inhabitants. I reacted, in some obscure way, against unfamiliarly liberal surroundings. This was my first view, from close up, of genuinely idyllic family life —and it was too much for me. Veronica and Maisie never fought. There seemed no way of driving a wedge between them. My Fiennes first cousins (Aunt Gertrude's children), to whom I was habituated, fought each other like demons, and I took part. (I learned, later, that owing to me the fighting grew worse.) No sooner was I happily into harbour with the Salmons than I started behaving like a yahoo: I sulked—lagging behind on walks, feigning loss of appetite at midday dinner. I bragged and exaggerated. Miss Clark considered me a typical only child, and said so. Mrs. Salmon, an acute, maternal, educated and resourceful gentlewoman, showed more patience: she observed me, thoughtful but with a knowledgeable twinkle in the eye. Occasionally she joined us in the schoolroom, augmenting or even taking over that day's lessons, and stimulating and fruitful those sessions were. *I* enjoyed them. I was at my best at lessons at that age— woolgatherings and abeyances came later. Betweentimes, we constructed a wonderful toy theatre, and staged a performance of *A Midsummer Night's Dream* (or, at least, of the Titania parts) with a cast of penny dolls glamorised by gauze. Or we sing-songed around the parish piano. Or Mrs. Salmon read aloud *The Talisman*. I could not have had less to complain of, one way and another: nothing was lacking—yet it was those very diversions which caught me out. A rift in the lute, a flaw in the crystal. . . . How trying *did* they find me? Probably they never allowed themselves to know. Mr. Salmon, whom I continued to idolise, sometimes swivelled upon me, from under jutting black eyebrows, a look of sardonic appreciation—satanic behaviour being, I suppose, in his line of country.

Possibly I was jealous of the whole family?

The sisters, with their animated, differentiated faces inside those contrasting cascades of hair (mine never grew longer than my shoulders), leaning together to look at the same book, strolling with arms interlaced, tying each other's sashes to go to parties (Veronica's sash sky-blue, Maisie's coral-pink). . . . While exasperating, they continued to charm me. I was told they felt an affection for me: *now* I see that, miraculously, they somehow did. But the fact was, sensibly or insensibly, I was missing Lindum, that larger, cruder theatre of action. There, we girls did not live actually the lives of gladiators, but by contrast with Old Cheriton we could seem to. Though a small school, it was a roomy world. One was not impinged upon. With notice-boards, hockey sticks, creaky desks, smelly inkpots, white mice stowed away in the cloakroom, catchwords, crazes and clatter, I was in my element: I was at that level. I was not fit, yet, to intake sweetness and light; the Old Cheriton foretaste came too early. This being either perceived by Mrs. Salmon and indicated to my mother, or perceived by my mother and indicated to Mrs. Salmon—or, possibly, dawning on both of ·them simultaneously?—lessons at the rectory terminated, in an atmosphere of unclouded amicability. I returned to Lindum; and my mother, there no longer being reason to live at Seabrook, began to mediate a return to Hythe, which would involve disengaging the furniture from Lyminge.

MY BELLIGERENCE, to a degree given an outlet, to a degree neutralised by school life, was inborn, a derivative of race. Irish and Anglo-Irish have it in common. It stood out, possibly, more strongly in the placidity of England. At times a tiresome trait, it is not a detestable one, being poles apart from aggressiveness—which as we know is engendered by some grudge, spite or bias against the rest of the world. Your belligerent person has no chip on his shoulder, and tends to sail through life in excellent spirits. He likes fighting. He distinguishes between a fight and a quarrel, on these grounds: a fight, soon over, purifies the air and leaves no one the worse (unless they are dead), whereas a quarrel, unlikely to be ever wholly resolved, not only fouls the surrounding air but may set up a festering trail of lifelong bitterness. That distinction has always been clear to me. I would go miles out of my way to avoid a quarrel.

Sir Jonah Barrington, to whose *Personal Sketches of His Own Times* I owe as all-round an account as I hope to find of the manners, tenets and general outlook on life of my ancestors, his compatriots and contemporaries, witnessed the regrettable decline of duelling in Ireland—where, as a manly practice, it had survived its all but extinction across the water. Cease to be lawful it might: a blind eye was turned to it. It was in the tradition, generic to that society which gave Sir Jonah and my relatives birth: the Ascendancy, with its passion for virtuosity of all kinds, not least sword-play or mastery with a pistol. In the best days, apparently, almost everyone fought:

Earl Clare, Lord Chancellor of Ireland, fought the Master of the Rolls, the Right Honourable John

Philpot Curran, with twelve-inch pistols. The Earl of Clonmel, Chief Justice of the King's Bench, fought Lord Tyrawly, about his wife, and the Earl of Landaff, about his sister; and others, with sword or pistol, on miscellaneous subjects. The Judge of the County of Dublin, Egan, fought the Master of the Rolls, Roger Barrett, and three others; one with swords. The Chancellor of the Exchequer, the Right Honourable Isaac Corry, fought the Right Honourable Henry Grattan, a privy counsellor, and the chancellor was hit. He also exchanged shots or thrusts with *two* other gentlemen. A baron of the exchequer, Baron Medge, fought his brother-in-law and two others—a hit. . . . The Judge of Prerogative Court, Doctor Duigenan, fought *one* barrister and frightened *another* on the ground. The latter was a very curious case. . . . The Provost of the University of Dublin, the Right Honourable Hely Hutchinson, fought Mr. Doyle, Master in Chancery: they went to the plains of Minden to fight. . . . The Right Honourable George Ogle, the Orange Chieftain, fought Barny Coyle, a whisky distiller, because he was a *papist*. They fired eight shots without stop or stay, and no hit occurred: but Mr. Ogle's second broke his own arm by tumbling into a potato-trench. . . .

Sir Jonah abridges, he says, "this dignified list," which, even so, takes up two of his pages: and I have further abridged it—his point is made. His attitude is, if nostalgic, reflective also: "It is nearly incredible what a singular passion the Irish gentlemen (though in general excellent-tempered fellows) had for fighting each other and immediately becoming friends again." Actually (we have it on his authority) a duel frequently served to cement a friendship. And why not? Did not the prestige date back to the chivalric tradition, to knightly jousting? —not really more honourable, and (should you not care for that sort of thing) just as futile? Semi-sacredness came to attach to family weapons: "Each family had its case of hereditary pistols, which descended as an heirloom." The Barringtons' were "included in the armoury of our ancient castle of Ballynakill in the reign of Elizabeth (the stocks, locks and hair-triggers were, however, modern). . . . One of them was named *'sweet lips'* the other *'the darling.'* " (One must not allow Sir Jonah to grate on one.) Sheridan, loosing Sir Lucius O'Trigger, in *The Rivals,* on to the modish—but in the Irish baronet's view, half-hearted—society of Bath, adds credibility to the Barrington jottings. Heiress-hunting (another national sport) does not occupy all Sir Lucius's time: he is master-minding Bob Acres into a duel. He is, however, riled by technical hitches—"I don't know what's the reason," he cries aloud, "but in England, if a thing of this kind gets wind, people make such a pother that a gentleman can never fight in peace and quietness."

Horsemanship apart, the Anglo-Irish, together with what was left of the indigenous autocrats, would subsequently have been in a poor way were it not for writing. To that we have taken like ducks to water. Accommodating ourselves to a tamer day, we interchanged sword-play for word-play. Repartee, with its thrusts, opened alternative possibilities of mastery. Given rein to, creative imagination ran to the tensed-up, to extreme situations, to confrontations. Bravado characterises much Irish, all Anglo-Irish writing: gloriously it is sublimated by Yeats. Nationally, we have an undertow to the showy. It follows that primarily we have produced dramatists, the novel being too life-like, humdrum, to do us justice. We do not do badly with the short story, "that, in a spleen, unfolds both heaven and earth" —or should. There is this about us: to most of the rest of the world we are semi-strangers, for whom existence has something of the trance-like quality of a spectacle. As beings, we are at once brilliant and limited; our unbeatables, up to now, accordingly, have been those who best profited by that: Goldsmith, Sheridan, Wilde, Shaw, Beckett. Art is for us inseparable from artifice: of that, the theatre is the home.

Possibly, it was England made me a novelist. At an early though conscious age, I was transplanted. I arrived, young, into a different mythology —in fact, into one totally alien to that of my forefathers, none of whom had resided anywhere but in Ireland for some centuries, and some of whom may never have been in England at all: the Bowens were Welsh. From now on there was to be (as for any immigrant) a cleft between my heredity and my environment—the former remaining, in my case, the more powerful. Submerged, the mythology of this "other" land could be felt at work in the ways, manners and views of its people, round me: those, because I disliked being at a disadvantage, it became necessary to probe. It cannot be said that a child of seven was analytic; more, with a blend of characteristic guile and uncharacteristic patience I took note—which, though I had at that time no thought of my future art, is, after all, one of the main activities of the novelist. At the outset, the denizens of England and their goings-on inspired me with what a hymn epitomises as "scornful wonder"—protective mechanism?—but I was not a disagreeable child, so any initial hostility wore off. Lacking that stimulus, my attention wandered: society not being by nature interesting, or for long interesting, to the very young, I transferred my gaze from it to its geographical setting. Thereafter, England affected me more in a scenic way than in any other—and still does. It was the lie of the land, with that cool, clear light falling upon it, which was extraordinary.

Well for me, that we pitched our camp where we did! Fortunate, I mean, that "England" was Kent, and, above all, Kent's dramatisable coastline. Suppose, for instance, some Cousin Lilla or Cousin Isabel had siren-sung us into the Midlands, with their soporific monotony? Or, for that matter, into the West Country, with its rainy semi-resemblances to Ireland? As it was, where we *were* stood out in absolute contrast to where we came from. Gone was the changing blue of mountains: instead, bleached blond in summer, the bald downs showed exciting great gashes of white chalk. Everything, including the geological formation, struck me as having been recently put together. Trees were smaller in size, having not yet, one could imagine, had time for growth. "Thunderbolts"—meteorites? —to be collected along the slippery dogpaths of the Warren might have rained down from the heavens the night before. And this *newness* of England, manifest in the brightness, occasionally the crudity, of its colouring, had about it something of the precarious. *Would* it last? The edifices lining the tilted streets or gummed at differing levels above the Channel seemed engaged in just not sliding about. How much *would* this brittle fabric stand up to? My thoughts dallied with landslides, subsidences and tidal waves.

England's appearance of youth was, however, gainsaid by evidences of history. Those were all over the place. In Ireland, history—because, I suppose, of its melancholy, uneasy trend—had on the whole tended to be played down; one knew *of* it, but spoke of it little. Here, it burst from under the contemporary surface at every point, arousing enthusiasm. A success story—or, in these days one might say, a gigantic musical. Everyone figured, including the Ancient Romans. Nor had any of the stage-sets for the performance—or, indeed, any of those rigged up for performances which had not,

after all, taken place, such as a Napoleonic invasion
—been cleared away: east of me Dover Castle,
shored up on tier-upon-tier of fortification, flew its
triumphant flag; west of me, martello towers diminished into the distance, more than one of them
pounded down into massive jumbles of broken
masonry, not, after all, by enemy cannon-fire but
by the sea, which had also breached the sea-wall,
for the elements had also taken a hand. Our Military Canal was not the less seductive for boating-
picnics for having as yet served no military purpose.
Foundations of circumspect-looking buildings were
(I heard) riddled with secret passages. The Cinque
Ports' navy had torn up and down the Channel
harassing any marauding French; smugglers had
cat-and-moused with revenue men over the marshes,
into the woods. To crown all, there had been terrific
marine pageantry, spectacular arrivals and departures, monarchs, brides, envoys and so on—a constant, glittering, affable come-and-go between here
and France. Not a dull moment.

"History" inebriated me, and no wonder.
Moreover, *here* was where it belonged: Kent-England had a proprietary hold on it. So it was this
landscape, with everything it was eloquent of and
comprehended, which won me (the newcomer to
it) over—filling me, at the same time, with envy
and the wish to partake. Not long after my eighth
birthday, celebrated at Folkestone, I entered upon
a long, voluptuous phase in which I saw life as a

non-stop historical novel, disguised only thinly (in my day) by modern dress. I saw myself, even, in an historic light, which gave at once a momentousness and a premonition of their possible consequences to all my doings. And the same attached to anyone who attracted me. When or how I divested myself of this daydream, I do not remember —did I entirely do so ever? Becoming a writer knocked a good deal of nonsense out of my system. But always there is a residuum. (I detect in my betters, the giants of my profession, a magnificent, self-exonerating silliness: would or could anybody become a novelist who was not internally silly in *some* way?) As a novelist, I cannot occupy myself with "characters," or at any rate central ones, who lack panache, in one or another sense, who would be incapable of a major action or a major passion, or who have not at least a touch of the ambiguity, the ultimate unaccountability, the enlarging mistiness of personages "in history." History, as more austerely I now know it, is not romantic. But I am.

ANOTHER LURE of this region's was architectural. When we got here, Edwardian villa-building, superimposed on the also pretty but stodgier late-Victorian, had for some years been at its most volatile and prolific. Dotted over hills in sight of the sea and in valleys out of it, villas came in all shapes— a phantasmagoric variety—and sizes. And not only were there villas but one could live in them—in

Ireland one could not: habit, fatalism or piety bound my people either to inherited homes or homes they had inherited ideas about, and almost unfailingly those were Georgian, box-square in the country, strait-and-narrow, with high front-door steps, in town. Onward from my birth (which took place in an intended back drawing-room at 15 Herbert Place), there had been an all but unbroken procession of similar rooms. Repetitive eighteenth-century interiors with their rational proportions and faultless mouldings, evenly daylit, without shadow, curiousness or cranny, not only said nothing to my imagination; they, if they did anything, repelled it. In so far as I found them anything I found them "sad," associating them perhaps with my father's illness. Outdoors, the uniformity of façades in Dublin (along streets terminated only by the horizon), and the inevitable alikeness of one landowner's mansion to another throughout the South, bespoke to me nothing but uninventiveness. I was surfeited with the classical when we sailed for England— where release, to the point of delirium, awaited me. I found myself in a paradise of white balconies, ornate porches, verandahs festooned with Dorothy Perkins roses, bow windows protuberant as balloons, dream-childish attic bedrooms with tentlike ceilings, sublimated ivory-fretwork inglenooks inset with jujubes of tinted glass, built-in overmantels with flight upon flight of brackets round oval mirrors, oxidized bronze door-handles with floral

28

motifs, archways demurely to be curtained across, being through-ways to more utilitarian or less mentionable parts of the dwelling, and so on. . . .

These were now to be mine. The prospect was heady. Villas we actually came to occupy were few (though, as already said, we did not do badly) in comparison with the hosts we viewed. This we mainly did, as my mother put it, "on chance." Any empty premises that we liked the look of we entered, whether at that time requiring or contemplating a change of residence or not. Part of the fun of the game was to obtain the key from the house agent without the house agent; occasionally our entrances were unauthorised—I became as adept as a Fagin pupil at snaking in through some forgotten little back window, then finding a door to unbolt to admit her. The deserted rooms, downstairs in summer often embowered in shadows of the syringa embowering the bewildered gardens, of which the lawns had grown high in hay, smelled intoxicatingly of wallpaper, sunshine, mustiness. With the first echo of our steps on the stripped floors, or of our voices excitedly hushed by these new acoustics, another dream-future sprang into being. We took over wherever we were, at the first glance. Yes, what a supposititious existence ours came to be, in these one-after-another fantasy buildings, pavilions of love. In the last of the villas in which it came about that we did actually live, she died.

Wobbly rustic steps led, often, up to a sagging terrace or down to a dried-out pool. Who *had* been the inhabitants, so mysteriously gone? I cannot wonder villas gained such a hold on me, waiting only a few years more to become the dominants of the stories I started to write. It being necessary there should be people to put in them, I summoned up "people": men, women, children. Much of my "creation" of character has, rather, been evocation, borne out by guesswork. Guesses have hit the mark, by a miracle.

How, though (at the time I am speaking of), did I reconcile my craze for—my infatuation with —villas, unhistorical gimcrack little bubbles of illusion, with my history-fed passion for the mighty, immortal and grandiose? I cannot say. The two ran concurrently.

And, of course, villas were part of the exoticism of Kent-England. They stood for an outing, a total contrast. Their frivolity chimed in with my fundamentally frivolous, semi-sceptical attitude to this "other" land. If you began in Ireland, Ireland remains the norm: like it or not. Looking through *Seven Winters,* which is about my earlier, Dublin childhood, I find I have said this: "I never looked up Sackville Street without pleasure, for I was told it was the widest street in the world. Just as Phoenix Park, grey-green distance beyond the Zoo, was the largest park in the world. These superlatives pleased me only too much: my earliest pride of race was

attached to them. And my most endemic pride in
my own country was, for some years, founded on a
mistake: my failing to have a nice ear for vowel
sounds, and the Anglo-Irish slurred, hurried way of
speaking, made me take the words 'Ireland' and
'island' to be synonymous. Thus, all other countries
quite surrounded by water took (it appeared) their
generic name from ours. It seemed fine to live in a
country that was a prototype. England, for instance,
was 'an ireland' (or, a sub-Ireland)—an imitation.
Then I learned that England was not even 'an ireland,' having failed to detach herself from the flanks
of Scotland and Wales. Vaguely, as a Unionist
child, I conceived that our politeness to England
must be a form of pity.

"In the same sense, I took Dublin to be the
model of cities, of which there were imitations scattered over the world."

I had yet to see London, when first we settled
in Kent. I had once or twice crossed it, for that was
necessary, but there had not been anything particularly metropolitan about our cab drives, usually
after dark and in a darkness which was generally
foggy, from one terminal railway station to another. In transit, we had called in on Cousin Bella
Guise, my mother's godmother, living in Cliveden
Place: but as Cousin Bella came from County
Wexford and had brought Wexford belongings and
their ambience with her, hers hardly was to be called
a London interior. How successful an imitation

31

of Dublin London was, I had not, therefore, so far been able to judge. Then, what about Folkestone? True, not a city but really a quite large town, my first English one. Folkestone, self-christened "Queen of the South," had hardly yet overdrawn on what had been a highly fashionable reputation. Henry James characters, for instance, had stayed there (though that I was not to know). Admittedly, Folkestone was *the seaside*—formerly associated by me with Anglesea lodging-houses, autumn changes-of-air. In the course of acclimatising to Folkestone, I looked round at it from the "imitation" angle. The place had wide, lengthy, raying-out avenues, tree-planted. The Leas—laid out as a high-up, sea-viewing promenade, up and down which sailed scarlet or pink silk parasols, tilted by owners glancing to see if one *could* see France—were handsome. Inland from the Leas was a hive of flourishing schools, of which mine was one. The shops were showy, and hummed with custom. Hotels were many, and some were gorgeous. Buildings either were of rubicund brick, with yellow-stone trimmings, or stucco, white, cream, pearl or dove-grey. Everywhere were hanging baskets of pink geraniums. Everything went well. In fact, I adapted to Folkestone (only to learn, alas, that my mother detested it). We removed to Hythe. I perceived in Folkestone an absolute, insulating self-contentment. Nothing other than Folkestone did it aspire to. An English "resort" versus the Irish Capital. The blotting-out of all my visual past was so total as to become giddying. What had to be bitten on was that two entities so opposed, so irreconcilable in climate, character and intention, as Folkestone and Dublin should exist simultaneously, and be operative, in the same life-time, particularly my own.

II

PLACES

FEW PEOPLE questioning me about my novels,
or my short stories, show curiosity as to the
places in them. Thesis-writers, interviewers or individuals I encounter at parties all but all stick to the
same track, which by-passes locality. On the subject
of my symbology, if any, or psychology (whether
my own or my characters'), I have occasionally
been run ragged; but as to the *where* of my stories,
its importance in them and for me, and the reasons
for that, a negative apathy persists.

Why? Am I not manifestly a writer for whom
places loom large? As a reader, it is to the place-
element that I react most strongly: for me, what
gives fiction verisimilitude is its topography. No
story gains absolute hold on me (which is to say,
gains the required hold) if its background—the
ambience of its happenings—be indefinite, abstract
or generalised. Characters operating *in vacuo* are
for me bodiless. Were I to meet a writer, living or
dead, whose work had so percolated into my own
experience as to become part of it, his places would

34

be what I should first want to discuss. How many—
I should desire to ask him—were "actual," how
many composed of fragmented memories (some
dating so far back as to be untraceable) organised
into shape? How many (were such a thing possible)
were *"imagined"* purely? How many structural alterations in a house, town or landscape otherwise
"actual" had to be made, to meet some unforeseen
exigency of the story's? And how often? Exactly
where are, or were, the originals (partial or in entirety) of places in this writer's narratives to be
found?

To me, questions of this kind are seldom
put.

One reason may be I am not a "regional"
writer in the accredited sense. Novelists being so
various and so many, it is necessary to assemble
them under headings, and under the "regional"
heading I am not placed: I do not qualify. The
Bowen terrain cannot be demarcated on any existing map; it is unspecific. Ireland and England,
between them, contain my stories, with occasional
outgoings into France or Italy: within the bounda-
ries of those countries there is no particular locality
I have staked a claim on or identified with. Given
the size of the world, the scenes of my stories are
scattered over only a small area; but they *are* scattered. Nothing (at least on the surface) connects
them, or gives them generic character of the kind
found to claim or merit consideration. Failing to

35

throw a collective light on my art, my places tend to be thought of as its accessories, engaging enough to read of but not "meaningful." Wherefore, Bowen topography has so far, so far as I know, been untouched by research. Should anyone give it a thought after I am dead, that will be too late. To it, only I hold the key.

When I say I am not a "regional" writer in the outright sense, do I mean that I am one in any other? Internally, yes. Since I started writing, I have been welding together an inner landscape, assembled anything but at random. But if not at random, under the influence of what? I suppose necessity, and what accompanies that. A writer needs to have at command, and to have recourse to, a recognisable world, geographically consistent and having for him or her a super-reality.

Lacking that, his or her art would be unconcrete, insulated and unconvincing—most fatal of all!—to the writer himself. For the "regionalist" proper, such a world is to hand: his native territory, plus its pre-natal hold on him. Acceptance, for him, is in itself inspiration; what could have been subjugation becomes victory. But it is necessary for him to be gigantic, as were for instance Hardy, Mauriac, Faulkner—and with that, stoical. Apart from not being on, or anywhere within sight of, the scale of those three, I have not in me the makings of regionalism as forged by them. Imagination of my kind is most caught, most fired, most worked upon by the unfamiliar: I have thriven, accordingly, on the changes and chances, the dislocations and (as I have said) the contrasts which have made up so much of my life. That may be why "my" world (my world as a writer) is something of a mosaic. *As* it is, it is something that assembled itself. Looking back at my work, I perceive that the scenes of my successive, various stories predetermined themselves. And not only that but they predetermined the stories to a greater extent than I may have known at the time.

A Quotation from "Notes on Writing a Novel"

Nothing can happen nowhere. The locale of the happening always colours the happening, and often, to a degree, shapes it. Scene, scenes . . . give the happening the desired force. . . . Scene is only justified in the novel where it can be shown, or at least felt, to act upon action or character. In fact, where it has dramatic use.

Where it is not intended for dramatic use, scene is a sheer slower-down. Its staticness is a dead weight. It cannot make part of the plot's movement by being shown *in play.* (Thunderstorms, the sea, landscape flying past car or railway-carriage windows are not scene but happenings.)

The deadeningness of straight and prolonged "description" is as apparent with regard to scene as it is with regard to character. Scene must be evoked. . . . Scene must, like the characters, not fail to materialise. In this it follows the same law—instantaneous for the novelist, gradual for the reader.

37

Though the "Notes" were contributed by me to John Lehmann's distinguished *Orion II* so far back as 1945, they contain nothing that now, years later, I would want to unsay (though I don't, now, like their peremptory tone). There are one or two statements I should be glad to expand, together with others I ought to qualify. The staticness of scene *is* a dead weight. Yes, indeed it can be; but there are ways round this. For instance, one can exploit the staticness—underline it, dramatise it effectively. That I had already done in *The House in Paris* (1935). Here is Mme. Fisher's sick-room as reacted to by the child Henrietta:

> Mme. Fisher's bedroom, though it was over the salon, had two windows, not one. Jalousies were pulled to over the far window, so that no light fell across the head of the bed. A cone of sick-room incense on the bureau sent spirals up the daylight near the door; daylight fell cold white on the honeycomb quilt rolled back. Round the curtained bedhead, Pompeian red walls drank objects into their shadow: picture-frames, armies of bottles, boxes, an ornate clock showed without glinting, as though not quite painted out by some dark transparent wash. Henrietta had never been in a room so full and still. She stood by the door Miss Fisher had shut behind her, with her heart in her mouth. Her eyes turned despairingly to a bracket on which stood spiked shells with cameos on their lips. The airlessness had a strange dry pure physical smell.
> "Here is Henrietta," Miss Fisher said.
> "Good morning, Henrietta," said Mme. Fisher.
> "Good morning, Mme. Fisher," Henrietta

replied. The hand she saw in the shadows did not stir on the sheet, so she stayed where she was on the parquet beside the door.

Staticness: the all-out of the dead weight. Yet this passage makes contradictory use of four vigorous anti-static verbs: "sent spirals up," "fell," "drank," "turned." It brings into the picture three (anti-static) lately completed acts: jalousies pulled to, quilt rolled back, door shut behind Henrietta. Further, there is an evocation of action thwarted (or withheld energy): light (because of the jalousies) does *not* fall across the head of the bed; ornate clock, glassy bottles, etc., show but "without glinting"; Mme. Fisher's hand does *not* stir on the sheet—though it could have. The one thing in action here is the incense cone consuming itself by its slow burning (and *it* is a sickness symbol). The room, felt by the child as "so full and still," is a case not of mere immobility but of immobilisation. In a terrible way, it is a *bois dormant*. What has brought this about? Mme. Fisher: on the bed in the centre.

Mme. Fisher was not in herself a pretty old lady. Waxy skin strained over her temples, jaws and cheekbones; grey hair fell in wisps round an unwomanly forehead; her nostrils were wide and looked in the dusk skullish; her mouth was graven round with ironic lines. Neither patience nor discontent but a passionate un-resignation was written across her features, tense with the expectation of more pain. She seemed to lie

39

as she lay less in weakness than in unwilling credulity, as though the successive disasters that make an illness had convinced her slowly, by repetition. She lay, still only a little beyond surprise at this end to her, webbed down, frustrated, or, still more, like someone cast, still alive, as an effigy for their own tomb.

SHE is the hub of the scene.

Alternatively, one can break the staticness down by showing scene in fluidity, in (apparent) motion. For that, the beholder must be in motion himself, on foot or on or in a conveyance of whatever kind, at whatever speed. The greater the speed, the more liquefying the process. He may be airborne—which is least satisfactory, for altitude flattens what is beneath. Better, he is traversing *terra firma,* by any of the many means, or on shipboard, moving across or along water: in both cases he then has the illusion of movement past him, or (should a ship be approaching a coast or a car making towards a range of mountains) towards him. He does not merely—as he would were he at a standstill—*see* scene, he *watches* its continuous changes, which act upon him compulsively like a non-stop narrative.

Here, for instance (again, from *The House in Paris*) is a ship, and on it, amongst others, a young woman. The crossing from a Welsh port has been overnight; just after dawn the ship turned in from the open sea, and is now making its way inland up the Lee River towards Cork city, where it will dock.

While Karen sat at breakfast in the saloon, trees began to pass the portholes; soon she went back on deck. The sun brightened the vapoury white sky but never quite shone: both shores reflected its melting light. The ship, checking, balanced uncertainly up the narrowing river, trees on each side, as though navigating an avenue, leaving a salt wake. Houses asleep with their eyes open watched the vibrating ship pass; against the woody background those red and white funnels must look like a dream. Seagulls, circling, settled on mown lawns. The wake made a dark streak in the glassy water; its ripples broke against garden walls. Every hill running down, each turn of the river, seemed to trap the ship more and cut off the open sea.

On the left shore, a steeple pricked up out of a knoll of trees, above a snuggle of Gothic villas; then there was the sad stare of what looked like an orphanage. A holy bell rang and a girl at a corner mounted her bicycle and rode out of sight. The river kept washing salt off the ship's prow. Then, to the right, the tree-dark hill of Tivoli began to go up, steep, with pallid stucco houses appearing to balance on the tops of trees. Palladian columns, gazebos, glass-houses, terraces showed on the background misted with spring green, at the top of shafts or on toppling brackets of rock, all stuck to the hill, all slipping past the ship.

Someone remarked, Bowen characters are almost perpetually in transit. Arguably: if you are to include transitions from room to room or floor to floor of the same house, or one to another portion of its surroundings. I agree, Bowen characters are in transit *consciously*. Sensationalists, they are able to re-experience what they do, or equally, what is done to them, every day. They tend to behold afresh and react accordingly. An arrival, even into another room, is an event to be registered in some way. When they extend their environment, strike outward, invade the unknown, travel, what goes on in them is magnified and enhanced: impacts are sharper, there is more objectivity. But then, is this not so with all persons, living or fictional? Simply, it may be, it is at such moments that men, women and children are by me most often portrayed.

I may, too, impart to some of my characters, unconsciously, an enthusiastic naïvety with regard to transport which in my own case time has not dimmed. Zestfully they take ship or board planes: few of them even are *blasés* about railways. Motor-cars magnetise them particularly. Bicycling, which is a theme-song in *A World of Love* and part of *The Little Girls,* began for me only when I was thirteen, after my mother's death. It had been the one activity she withheld me from, her professed reason being that child cyclists grew up with bandy legs—her inner one could have been the fate of Aubrey, one of my early confederates at Hythe, flung to his death in an accident one fine morning. . . . Aunt Laura, with whom I went to live at Harpenden, was herself seldom off a bicycle, so was calmer: once she considered me competent, she procured for me a glittering brand-new Raleigh. "Now *this* is yours," she said. First riding the Raleigh, I dismounted, often, simply to stand and look at it. This, my first machine, had an intrinsic beauty. And it opened for me an era of all but flying, which roads emptily crossing the airy, gold-gorsy Common enhanced. Nothing since has equalled that birdlike freedom.

In a way, as a writer I may be at an advantage in being born when I was. Not born, that is, into the age of speed, I was there while it came into being round me: much that went on was new not only to me but wholly new in itself, by its own right. About motor-cars and their offspring motor-bikes there continued, for longer than may be realised now, to be something mythical and phenomenal—even hostile? "Flying machines," at the start were less ill-seen: few and freakish, they constituted a threat only to aeronauts who took off in them. Motor-cars, which spawned at a greater rate, looked at once Martian and caddish. Their colour spectrum and flashing fittings of brass were themselves offensive. The combustion engine, with its splutterings and roarings, was at once disagreeable and enigmatic. . . . The age of speed, thus exemplified, was not—at least by Folkestone and its surroundings, fair cross-section of *rentier* civilisation—cordially welcomed in: recollect that it superimposed itself upon an existing age, a state of society, which *had,* already, all it consciously wanted. Thanks to the previous century's revolutionising discovery, steam power, there by now was suave, trustworthy, comfortable locomotion, rapid enough: trains, steamers. And existence was further enhanced by a host of amenities: telephones, electric light, electric bells, lifts, gramophones, pianolas. There were occasional moving-picture shows. The twentieth century, therefore, dawned on a world which already had cause to regard itself as completely modern, and congratulate itself thereupon. Enough was enough. Anything further, one felt, might annoy God.

Propaganda against speed went out to children. One line of attack called it "against nature." Its intensifications, however, *we* were to discover, were good for art. As I say, speed is exciting to have grown up with. It alerts vision, making vision retentive with regard to what only may have been seen for a split second. By contrast, it accentuates the absoluteness of stillness. Permanence, where it occurs, and it does occur, stands out the more strongly in an otherwise ephemeral world. Permanence is an attribute of recalled places.

SCHOOLS—as I knew them—crystallised place-feeling.

Harpenden Hall, second of the three I went to, was the most comely. Built, I should think, in the late seventeenth century, low, long, graceful and solid, "The Hall" stood a short way back from the bicycling Common, on to which its windows gazed calmly out. In front, a paved path led to it, across lawns. It looked like a picture in a romantic novel with a historic trend. (I did, in fact, and while I was still there, come on a black-and-white of it in a

44

Louis Wain Annual, the great cat artist having resided in Harpenden during at least some of his years of fame.) Indoors, the panelling of the main rooms was a dimmed ivory, the steps of the dark polished staircase were shallow. Where there was not panelling there were Morris wallpapers. This did not look like a school.

But then, neither had Lindum done so, nor would Downe House. Never had I the misfortune to be educated in any building erected for that purpose. Each of my schools being small (I believe, by choice), each had established itself, with minimal changes, in what had till recently been a private house. The effect was a genial air of make-do—reassuring to an anti-scholastic child. At Harpenden Hall, the now desk-filled ivory parlours and bare-floored dining-room with "gym" apparatus fitted around its walls kept the climate of earlier, "ordinary" occupation. Or here and there vanished tribes left frivolous traces, or sentimental ones—names cut on the glass of windows. . . . This did not distract our attention, which was demanded. We *learned:* the classrooms were brisk, the teaching was thorough. No one of the schools I went to was amateurish.

On the surface only—that touch of improvisation—did any resemble St. Agatha's, in *The Little Girls:*

Thick cream glazed blinds were pulled most of the way down. Failing to keep out the marine sunshine, they flopped lazily over the open windows in the hot June breath rather than breeze haunting the garden. St. Agatha's had been a house, IV-A classroom probably the morning-room. The blinds were lace-bordered. There was a garlanded wallpaper—called to order by having on it a bald, pontifical clock, only a size or two smaller than a station one, a baize board clustered with lists and warnings, and sepia reproductions of inspiriting pictures, among them "Hope," framed in oak. Of oak were the desks, to which were clamped high-backed seats. An aroma of Plasticene came from the models along the chimneypiece, and from jars of botanical specimens near a window whiffs of water slimy with rotting greenery were fanned in—the girl in charge of the specimens being absent with one of her summer colds. Chalk in the neighbourhood of the blackboard and ink thickening in china wells in the desks were the only other educational smells.

A dozen or so girls, most of them aged eleven, some ten, some twelve, sat at the desks. All wore their summer tunics of butcher-blue.

St. Agatha's is imaginary, in that it has no physical origin. No link, for instance, with real-life Lindum, apart from both being girls' day-schools in a Kent seaside town. St. Agatha's, you recall, had its own beach, together with uphill "grounds"; Lindum, built in to a close residential area, was neither in view nor in easy reach of the sea. . . . Yet I perceive fictitious St. Agatha's with the same detailed, stereoscopic clearness as that with which I recollect solid Lindum. In the long run, art is realler than life? St. Agatha's *has* one link with Harpenden

Hall, for a school garden in Hertfordshire (not Kent) was the scene of an act that survives in *The Little Girls.*

I ENTERED Harpenden Hall, at mid-term, still in a state of shock. It was something to find myself making a fresh start. The less said the better: I had what I see can go with total bereavement, a sense of disfigurement, mortification, disgrace. The more people who had never met me before, the better. Though inevitably a number of Harpenden people would know *about* me: my popular uncle and aunt's having a little niece coming to live with them, and the reason for that, would have been broadcast. ("Little," I had come to notice, was part of the vocabulary of pathos—if a baby died, it was always a "little" baby.) Would the Harpenden Hall girls have been told about my disaster? As to that I did not know what to wish. Sometimes I wanted non-entity, sometimes celebrity.

Those wishes came uppermost alternately. Result, ambivalence in the matter of the school uniform. The uniform itself I particularly liked—I was all for it, and saw it likely to be a becoming one: brown tunic box-pleated into a square yoke (exactly as today) with a blue-and-white striped shirt to be worn under it, and a brown tie to be knotted over the shirt.

This outfit was, thanks to forethought, ready for me when I arrived at Harpenden, and I could

47

not wait to be into it, to be "merged." But I insisted on wearing a *black* tie. I did not, now it came to the point, wish to be stripped of my insignia. Since my mother's death, in September, I had worn mourning, of the euphemistic kind permitted for children; black, while not ever total, had not ever been missing and had spoken out, like the ink of a notice-board, from whatever part of my person it was on. *Now,* and so soon, was I to be shorn of that? "My black" was the last I had of my mother. *That* gone, there would be nothing, so far as I knew, ever again. For I could not remember her, think of her, speak of her or suffer to hear her spoken of.

Aunt Laura, no less in a state of shock, said, "Just as you like"; 1912 (which this still was) had been an unbearable year. The closeness of the Colleys to one another, the depths of their involvement with one another, magnified anything that might happen: and see what had! That March handsome clever Constance, the woman doctor, consumptive, had died in a Folkestone nursing home, on her way back from an unavailing Swiss sanatorium. That April Eddy, the youngest and dearest brother, had gone down with the *Titanic.* That summer Florence, my mother, was told by a Dublin doctor, to her delight, that she would be in Heaven six months hence. (It was to be less than six months.) We returned to Kent where my father joined us. That September the evenings at Hythe, even up on the hill, were stuffy and bodeful. The sorts of evenings

48

which later one associated with the thrummings of a bomber, circling, coming brutally nearer each time. She died, at Clyne House, on the ——— of the month. I was staying next door.

The problem I represented had been solved in advance: I was to go to Aunt Laura. My mother had made the arrangement with loving optimism, and Aunt Laura accepted it as a vocation. Considering all she had been through, that three-death year, might not having me to cope with have been the finish? As against that, may the challenge have braced her up? At all events, the energy, ingenuity and briskness with which she rose to the occasion did her credit in the eyes of the rest of the family, inclined till then to refer to her as "poor Laura," on the grounds of her being a shade sentimental, unmarried, and muddle-headed, and of having been down-trodden by her more brilliant sisters—not least Florence. . . . The actual sufferer under the arrangement could have been Uncle Wingfield, the angelic unmarried clergyman brother for whom, at this time, at Harpenden, she kept house. His prolonged bachelor state was said to be due to her zealous chaperonage. He, a winning, delightful man, was with regard to some aspects of life pathologically shy, bashful, prone to cramping embarrassments. Still being a curate, though an important one, he did not as yet qualify for a parsonage: South View, a semi-detached villa, already contained, to a nicety, his entourage: Aunt Laura, their "working housekeeper" Miss Kilby, and the dog Susan. The wedging-in, on top of these, of a girl supposedly on the verge of puberty, could have spelled for him more than spatial discomfort. His sweetness of nature, however, triumphed. He was forever devising "surprises" for me: treats, gifts, jokes, outings. All of these were accompanied by an understanding speechlessness, which I valued. If any gout or driblet of love—of affection, even— was during that time to be wrung from my petrified heart, it was for him. . . . But South View was in great part wasted on me. I did not desire "a home life," the fact was. It would have been better to send me straight to boarding-school. I made do by devoting myself to Harpenden Hall, where I spent about ten hours of each day.

Getting me in there had been a coup of Aunt Laura's. The school did not want to take any more day-girls: in intention, since it began, it had been a boarding-school, and Miss English wished it to keep that character. However, her objections were overborne. Two or three weekly boarders were there, from neighbouring parts of Hertfordshire; *the* boarders all, but all, came from London. At Lindum, day-school pure and simple, my fellow-girls had necessarily been "locals": one could track any one of them back to her home surroundings— which in the end could wither one's interest.

Londoners were birds of another feather. In uniform, they had the look of being in disguise—

who knew what they wore in the capital city? Collectively they were characters in the stage sense, or in the novel's, of whom the entirety never is to be known—or, if known, told. They were a breed I had not been among before. I attributed to them foreign splendours and miseries, and why not? At this juncture, this lifeless time in my own life, something outstanding and startling was what I needed: these girls *had* to be out of the ordinary run. Whether they were or were not, I cannot now say. They were ever so slightly sophisticated, compared to me and my fellow Harpenden day-girls, but not depraved. They were known in the village, drifting shopping around in their Hall tunics, as being old-for-their ages. They had as models, probably, social mothers. Two were nascent beauties: Dorothy Lewis, of mysterious (and, it was to transpire, sensational) parentage, whose short, dazzling subsequent life and terrible death outdid the utmost I could have foreseen for her; and Agatha Kentish, "a big girl," golden to the tips of her eyelashes, serene but given to the loveliest blushing—where is *she* now? Also among our numbers were two foreigners: Lili, my first German, from Düsseldorf, Junoesque, pink-and-white, good-humoured though with a disparaging smile; and Françoise, from where in France I do not remember, bilious complexion, darting berry-dark eyes, sharp elbows, topknot of hair upheld by a vast black bow like a flapping raven. *Her* smile was quizzical, rallying, just not cynical. When the First World War broke out, in 1914, those two were my prototypes of the warring nations. The War had the tact to break out during school holidays.

Harpenden Hall, as said, was a good school. The teaching was calm and authoritative. We were kept abreast of what went on in the world. What I learned there has—as by now, how could it not?— subsided into the compost which is the base of one's mind; but I know I did learn. Unhappily there was at that time little to show for it. At Lindum, I had been on the whole a bright child: quick answerer, fluent if moralistic essayist, comer-out-top at spelling, general knowledge, even mental arithmetic. Now the bright child gave place to the dunce girl. When, every Monday morning, after school prayers, Miss English read out to the assembled school the form-orders of the preceding week, I came out bottom or bottom-but-one of mine. To save my face, I adopted a pose of being "lazy." This must have been chagrinning for Miss English, upon whom, I suspect, I had been imposed by Aunt Laura as eager, intelligent and "promising." She had the grace to show herself as less vexed than puzzled. One or two of the mistresses took against me, saying I sulked. My defection did me little harm with the girls, one of whom said, "But you must be clever in *some* way."

My stupidity may have been due to denied sorrow. Officially, since I was then thirteen, it could have been charged—as it certainly would be these days—to an overpowering onslaught of adolescence. That would have been incorrect. I never did have adolescence at all badly, either at Harpenden Hall or at Downe House. Chicken-pox, measles, German measles, mumps, whooping-cough in turn took their toll of me, and heavily, but with the last of those my afflictions ceased. Adolescence apparently by-passed me—or if I ever did have it, I got off light. Towering periods of silliness, oh yes. And I made vile scenes with unfortunate Aunt Laura, but those were, rather, instances of protracted childhood, which a furious selfishness reinforced. At around sixteen I dabbled in introspection, but hardly more. Tormenting nameless disturbances, conflicts, cravings were not experienced by me. I had never heard of them.

I would have been more galled by intellectual failure had I not had an alternative foot to stand on. I'd become a high-ranking initiator of school crazes, for which there was constant demand at Harpenden Hall. One or two had been going when I arrived, at mid-term, but showed signs of being upon the wane. Further ideas and impetus were needed: mine filled the bill. In a short time I had zealots excavating for secret passages, one at least of which was said, I can't say by whom, to run from The Hall cellars to the doubtless bone-strewn vaults of the parish church away off at the other end of the village. The cellars were tortuous, endless, musty and, at a first reconnaissance, unrewarding: evidently our end of the passage had been blocked up, by some malignant hand. We first tapped then beat about with our trowels along the walls, dislodging segments of scabrous plaster, harkening for "hollownesses." I carried a tottering candle; the London boarders were to a girl equipped with electric torches, procured by them for nightly reading in bed—lurid historical romances—after Lights Out. This (had we known) not really very original Gothic experiment of ours was put a stop to: our bangings-about had been audible upstairs; the cobwebs and coal dust in which we emerged coated caused unfriendly remarks. So next we moved onward to the occult. Marjory Bowen's *Black Magic* became our bible, though we gleaned what we could about witchcraft, demonic possession and the technique of cursing also from lesser works. At first we were at a loss for anybody to curse; the least popular member of the staff, an aggressive carrot-haired Scotswoman, was at length decided on, and the ceremonial of wax-image modelling, then pin-sticking, gone through. Miss X promptly came out with a "runny" cold, which she gave to us all—for fuller results we had needed fingernail clippings, plus one or two of her dreadful hairs. Lack of major ingredients, bats' blood, etc., also told against the potions we brewed, though we moaned incantations. Dorothy Lewis wanted to woo the Devil, but he remained away— which was as well, for cumulatively this thing was making us nervous: one of the girls began to shriek in her sleep, two or three who were about to be confirmed developed scruples and I began to have qualms about Uncle Winkie. So we gave over and started collecting perchy-birds. A village shop had an aviary-full of them: they were miniature bright-painted celluloid imitations of exotic species from many parts of the world. Each cost a penny. Each had a weight in its tail, enabling it to perch upright wherever placed—table-edge, bedhead, taut cord or outstretched finger. Flicked at, they swayed to and fro, not ceasing to perch. Their delicate equilibrium besotted us. Borne round in a dandified manner, as though falcons, they were caressed and murmured to: banished, inevitably, from classrooms they were all the more a feature of school walks: we sported them, when we filed from Harpenden Hall—semi-transparent in sunshine, brilliant as emblems—stuck rail-down into the rims of our knitted caps. . . . Then *they* ceased: *they* might never have been. We had had enough of them.

Gambling with death was instigated by Eileen Carver, whose unwilling lieutenant I became. We entered upon a carnival of bravado, or alternatively incipient commando training, wall-top running, roof-top running, roof mountaineering (the roofs of the Hall were steep) and blindfold bicycling being the early stages. She was a small, taut, pale, wiry London girl, alarmingly taciturn, demon at basketball (at which she captained us) and not basketball only. She had ruthlessly slighted the rest of our crazes, so far. A withheld personality, apt to become a searing one. Afternoon "nature rambles" over Harpenden Common or through hitherto friendly Hertfordshire thickets and lanes became, that autumn, darkened by apprehension: what might not she challenge us to do next? When it came to balancing, at a run, *eyes shut,* along the sky-high parapet of a railway bridge, several defaulted. She did not so much as look at them. Worst was to be the day of the deadly nightshade—for as that a spray of berries glistening under a hedge was identified by two embryonic botanists. "If *you* eat those, if you even touch those, you die!" "Rot," returned our Leader, in her most languid tone. "How do you know it's rot?" She flickered those summing-up eyes from face to face, then said: "Well, all right—at least *I* am." She plucked a palmful of berries and gulped them down.

Throughout school tea, choked, we awaited the onset of the convulsions: after-tea prep, clamped in rows to our desks, captive spectators, spying upon the stealthy advance of the wall clock, glancing away from the clock at her bullet-head, *we* were the immolated ones. "What's the *matter* with you all?" thundered Miss X, our invigilator that evening—"eh?" So we acted writing, scratch-scratch-scratch with our pens, or reading, holding books up to our faces. Then a girl clapped a hand to her mouth and ran out, to vomit. I was the only

56

day-girl in that classroom: at six-thirty Miss X ordered me home. So *I* deserted: back on the Raleigh to South View.

"Is deadly nightshade fatal?" I asked Aunt Laura. She said, so she had always supposed, adding: "Why?"

Next morning, Eileen was very well.

We then switched to collecting crêpe-de-Chine hankies, of every colour, these costing sixpence each. At Harpenden Hall (I repeat) took place the "burying" which centralises *The Little Girls*. The real-life proceedings were less impressive, more scatterbrained, and had a tinge of facetiousness. A smallish biscuit tin, sealed, containing some cryptic writings and accompanied by two or three broken knick-knacks, was immured in the hollow base of a rough stone wall dividing the kitchen garden: this taking place, I think, at about the time of our failure to uncover the secret passage. Foiled of the past, we at least might make a fool of the future. This attempt I had completely forgotten till it was returned to me by *The Little Girls*.

III

PEOPLE

No one of the characters in my novels has originated, so far as I know, in real life. If anything, the contrary was the case: persons playing a part in my life—the first twenty years of it—had about them something semi-fictitious. Born with no idea what people are like, I was slow to learn, therefore made guesses at them. A guess is an exercise of inventiveness. Some of my guesses may not have been quite wide of the mark—but if that was so, it was so by fortuity. Those concerned, whether grown-ups or children, either did not perceive what was going on or did not object to it: it is something to have "character" attributed to one, of whatever kind. For a main trait of human nature is its amorphousness, the amorphousness of the drifting and flopping jellyfish in a cloudy tide, and secret fears (such as fear of nonentity), discouragement and demoralising misgivings prey upon individuals made aware of this. There results an obsessive wish to acquire outline, to be unmistakably demarcated, to *take shape*. Shape—shape is the desideratum: hence the overlordship of characters in novels, who have it, over the desirous reader who has it not. Fictional characters stand out, enlarged by doing so. That their power is given them by art does not (indeed, must not) appear. They *are:* thereby, their effect is tonic.

I do not think my make-believe about people was peculiar as a future novelist: friends I have who have never written a line tell me, as children they did the same. But I ask myself, could those early dodges of mine queer the pitch for me as an autobiographer? What *was,* as opposed to what I chose to imagine, is what I want to unearth: long-ago actualities are the exciting thing—the more so for their being hard to discern clearly thanks to patchy surviving mists, the debris of childhood. To the fraction of the past that is in my keeping, I should like to give the sobriety of history: facts, events, circumstances demand to be accurately re-corded: that is my aim. But, people?—the denizens of those times and places? With people, the impos-sibility of "accuracy" begins. Those I lived among and therefore know to have lived, after all and by the end of it all, what were they? Many, and by now I suppose most of them, having taken their mysteries to the grave with them, I cannot ask them. Gone, they remain—elusive as ever.

With the characters in my stories it has been

otherwise. Between them and me existed, exists, no gulf. I could say, they have made themselves known to me—instantly recognisable, memorable from then on. From the moment they hove into view, they were inevitable. Nominally "imaginary," these beings made more sense, were more convincing, more authoritative as humans, than those others, consisting of flesh-and-blood, that I had wasted years in failing to know. These newcomers (for their visitations began only when, at twenty, I began to invoke them by writing stories) inspired me with what had been a lacking confidence: I gained, I grew, I assimilated much from being on terms with them, for they were adult as compared to myself— in experience, for instance, far, far ahead of me. They enlightened me, I believe, as to many things. I became, and remain, my characters' close and intent watcher: their director, never. Their creator I cannot feel that I was, or am. Yet in spite of all that, they were my servitors, for it was within *my* stories (stories conceived by me) that they existed, being in being only that they might play their assigned parts. I thought of stories first, of characters afterwards. . . . For some time, I did not draw heavily on my characters, for the reason that I kept to writing short stories, some of them very short, hardly more than sketches: I was a visual writer, with no taste for analysis, so those suited me better—my first two books, *Encounters* and *Ann Lee's,* were collections of them.

[*Here the ms. breaks off. She had, however, prepared, some while earlier, notes about the book for her publishers and these give some idea of the themes she at that time had in mind for the later sections.* S.C.B.]

It is not easy to make a synopsis of this (projected) book—of which the title is drawn from page 1 of *Alice's Adventures in Wonderland*. Much of the life, or liveliness, of the book should derive from its sparking its way along by free association— "recalls," and the ideas a recall brings with it.

The book is *not* to be an autobiography. It will differ from an autobiography (in the accepted sense) in two ways. (1) It will not follow a time sequence. (2) It will be anything but all-inclusive.

The underlying theme—to which the book will owe what it is necessary that a book *should* have, continuity—will be the relationship (so far as that can be traceable, and perhaps it is most interesting when it is apparently not traceable) between living and writing. Dislike of pomposity inhibits me from saying, "the relationship between life and art" (meaning my own).

The book is to be illustrated by quotations.

Some, from books by other people. So far as I am able to foresee, these will be very largely from "old" books, of which the copyright has expired. If there are exceptions, they will be brief.

Other quotations will be from books by me. The use of quotations from my own books will not be a sign of laziness on my part. The quotations will be used to give point and relevance to, and to illustrate, what in this new book I shall be in course of saying. It would seem to me stupid, and in a way dishonest, to rewrite, or paraphrase, anything I have already written—and published.

ONE OF MY REASONS for wishing to write this book (*Pictures and Conversations*), and one, also, why I think it should be a fairly good or at least an engaging book, is: books, lengthy critical studies, theses are perpetually being written about writers, novelists in particular. I, inevitably, have been the subject of a certain number of these. While appreciative of the honour done me and of the hard work involved, I have found some of them wildly off the mark. To the point of asking myself, if anybody *must* write a book about Elizabeth Bowen, why should not Elizabeth Bowen?

Structure of Pictures and Conversations

I foresee the book as dividing itself into five sections.

I. ORIGINS. My own: Anglo-Ireland and its peculiarities. The infiltration—I believe?—of at least some of these peculiarities into my books. This documented by the Jonah Barrington memoirs, Le Fanu and Edgeworth novels, and others.

II. PLACES. Their sometimes fateful influence. The sometimes contrasts, sometimes affinities between them. The topography of Elizabeth Bowen fiction.

III. PEOPLE. (a) in "real life": some famous, others obscure.

(b) in novels and stories I have written.

The inevitable question, where do "characters" come from?

IV. GENESIS (of a book, in particular of a novel or long short story). Remarks on the growth a book makes while being written. Remarks, also, on the subsequent growth a book makes when, having been published, and the cable having been cut between it and the author, it enters upon an unforeseeable life of its own.

V. WITCHCRAFT: A QUERY. Is anything uncanny involved in the process of writing? General conclusions drawn by the author, with regard in part to her own work, but also no less, if anything more, to that of the hierarchy of other writers.

Added to this, a page or so winding up *Pictures and Conversations.*

I can think of nothing further to add to this— I can see—rather sketchy forecast of *Pictures and Conversations.* I shall know more about this book when I am under way with it. A considerable—in fact, probably the greater—part of what it *is* to be about is still fairly deep down in my consciousness, waiting to be brought to the surface.

The Move-In

*(Chapter I of the unfinished novel
on which she was working when she died)*

THE MOVE-IN took place on a stuffy July evening. A car, open two-seater of some former
day, zigzagged its way up the steep approach to
a house, panting with exhaustion. Below lay a
large lake. In front were the driver and a friend;
behind the youths, and above them, a girl sat on the
folded-back hood—maintaining balance, at each of
the hairpin bends, by clutching at the scalp of one
or other of her companions. The car had a dicky
seat, but it not only looked unsafe but was too
lonely: it was occupied therefore by such baggage
as had failed to be fitted into the boot—bursting
plastic mesh bags, a raffia-embroidered basket of
unknown origin containing clothing, and bundles of
other clothing, rolled up in a newspaper, were pre-
vented from falling off by string.

The car had been followed uphill by flies and
midges, and more kept emerging, to join the party,
out of the honeysuckle, brambles and buzzing
bracken. Nobody spoke.

The house, as they neared it, disappeared from

view. However, it was unable to escape them. There it still had to be, like it or not, when finally they drove out on to the gravel—a sort of terrace overlooking the lake. The house, whatever its possibilities, looked ugly: it probably had been built for some sporting purpose. Its front was matted with creepers, from which rose gables; each side of the porch a bay window bulged forward on to the gravel. Out one side ran an additional wing, though with shutters shut. The porch door stood open; so did some windows.

The terrace parapet was overhung by fuchsias —the driver sidled the car some distance along it before the engine came to a natural stop. There remained no sound other than that of the water boiling in the radiator. Simply by sitting where they were, the three commanded a line of vision into the dining-room: in there, in the dusk, people appeared to be seated around a table, which, unless they were holding a séance or playing cards, meant a meal in progress. Though it could be that they were holding a séance, for a white patch, similar to a wisp of ectoplasm, was in motion. With their eyes the watchers followed this for some time: the phenomenon proved to be only one degree less occult than they had supposed. The cap of a parlourmaid. . . . The species, so far as they knew, had been long extinct.

The cap paused, somewhere back in the dark. The maid, disembodied by having no apron over her black garb, must be stealing a look, from her distance, out of the window. No other notice however was being taken—the meal went on. Indeed, if the persons eating were not stopped, there was danger that they might devour everything. The girl, to whom the danger had first occurred, urgently dug with a foot at her two companions, one of whom then got out of the car. He advanced to the porch and gave a tug at a bell.

Waiting, he saw some way into the hall. An opened telegram, two close-written pages, lay on a table beside a gong, though from where he was standing he could not read it. Then out of the dining-room came a woman, who hesitated, then shut the door behind her, with what somehow was malicious intent. Far from young, she did not seem best pleased—though she turned on him the exasperating expression of someone habituated to being pleasant. "Yes?" she said, and waited. She then added: "The bell doesn't ring."

"We supposed you saw us," he said severely.

"Well, we did, but we thought perhaps it was a mistake. People sometimes do come up here by mistake, or to see what there is, or look at the view; then they go away again. Sometimes we are in the middle of dinner."

"So we saw," he said sternly.

She looked down at herself and plucked a bur from her jersey, murmuring, "So *we* saw." The virulent violet shaggy jersey, a form of jacket, was not more than draped or huddled around her shoulders: the unoccupied sleeves of it, dangling down, had the look of additional arms. She twiddled, also, a pair of fancy spectacles, which she put on, the better to take a look at him, then took off again. "Although of course," she said, "if there's really anything—?"

"Yes, there is," he told her. "That is—is this house yours?"

"So far as I know."

"Then I think I am a friend of your nephew's."

"No, that I am afraid you can't be. Nobody could be."

"Why, what's so wrong with *him?*" he demanded hotly.

"He doesn't exist. I haven't got a nephew. I've never had one."

"Oh."

"I'm sorry, but there it is. What was his name?"

"Simon," he said, still deeply aggrieved.

"Where did you meet him?"

"On a bus in Spain. He advised me to look you up—that is, if I ever thought of coming to the West. He said you would always provide a base."

"A what?"

"Beds, and so on. He said it would cheer you up."

"He did not happen to mention his aunt's name?"

"He wrote it down on some envelope, but I lost it."

"His aunt just lives in the West, like Young Lochinvar?"

"There seemed to be some address, but I lost the envelope."

"What was *his* name?"

"Simon," he said unshakably.

"No, but his other?"

"I don't suppose he said. He got off the bus."

"I see." She clasped herself by the throat. "What I don't see is, what brought you *here?*"

That he could tell her. "Asking. From what he said, you lived on top of a lake, so when we sighted the lake we began asking. That was, we started asking the natives for someone of around your age and description. All of them seemed to think that should be you—that is, all of them sent us here."

"Fiends!" she cried out. "Devils incarnate!"

At this the dining-room door, as though only waiting, cautiously opened—at least an inch. Through, from a mouth in the aperture, came a plaintive voice. "Agatha? Agatha, the *soufflé*—it's going down!"

"Eat it, then," retorted the so-called Agatha, as an aside, bitterly, "you two!"

"Well, we are doing that, in a way, but we thought of you."

"Go away, Laura."

The person, going away with dejected steps,

contrived to leave open the inch of door. The woman Agatha realised this to be so: from now on, resistance began to stiffen. "There are other lakes," she told him. "Look at your map."

"Other lakes are not much use at this time of night."

"Oh, they're all quite near! Still, you ought to get going."

"Going?" he asked warily, with a frown.

"To wherever it is. To somewhere else."

"That is not so simple," he said, "as you seem to think."

Further disturbance came, from inside the dining-room. The voice this time, although male of a kind, was more agitated and tense than the one before. "Agatha—we think something is happening!"

"Coming, coming!"

"No, but do look *outside!*"

This porch, where the parley was being held, looked on nothing but sky and a bit of gravel—the woman however was out of it, out-of-doors, in two strides; and the youth, lest she elude him, followed. She had put on her spectacles and stood staring, slowly tying the sleeves into a knot, which she drew tighter, across her stony and unrewarding chest. "Your friends," she asked, "exactly what are they doing?"

Could she not see? They were unpacking the car.

72

"They think this is it, you see," the leader explained.

Round where the car was, near the dining-room window, the terrace was now a scene of activity. Naturally bored by the long wait, his friends were ahead with work on the dicky—once disencumbered, that could be tipped up, to allow for emptying of the boot. There had not been a basic clearance for some days: this evening, start of a lengthy stay, had been deemed to be an occasion for one. Gaping mesh bags, dumped, one by one heeled over, shedding forth their contents; shirts awaiting a dip writhed over the gravel. A lidless pot of ointment for skin irritants, a half-eaten banana thriftily folded back into its skin, a trodden-on wrist watch and a wing off a seagull lodged, for the time being, on a back mudguard. The girl, her small tight blue bottom towards the onlookers, was at the moment squinting under the car to make certain nothing had rolled away. Her comrade shook dust from a jerkin, then from a raincoat, then spread both garments over the fuchsia parapet.

The scene had a second audience, placed more favourably. In the bay of the dining-room, framed by adjoining windows, stood a man, livid with consternation, and a woman in what only could be hysterics—her handkerchief darted from her eyes to the tip of her nose, down to her mouth, then back to her eyes to start on its round again; and she rocked slightly.

73

"This *is* a mistake, I'm afraid," said the woman Agatha. She gathered herself together and added: "Stop them!"

At that, the girl turned round. She stood, took a stare at the woman, then said, somewhat moodily: "Hullo." She was smallish, young, wore rolled-up jeans and a man's shirt two or three sizes large for her. Tow-blonde hair, unequally short, dripped forward; a bramble-slash gave some sort of expression to a face mute and blank with temper and bleached by dust. Shifting her stare to the young man, she asked: "What are you standing there for?"

He said: "She says she is not his aunt."

"She what?"

"She says she has never heard of him."

"Well, that's not my fault," said the girl. "I can't help that. Anyway, here we are."

"Well, *she* says we're not," he unwillingly said, with a glance at Agatha. Slowly, with tigerlike motions down from the elbow, the girl tore at the bites on one of her arms, then on the other. She licked or sucked away one or two beads of blood, then thought. She looked away at the lake, up at the sky, threateningly at the house, more so at the watchers in the windows. She at last said: "We have to be somewhere, don't we? Haven't you told her?"

"I told her it isn't as simple as all that." Gored, at last, into action, he faced the hostess. "The thing is, we can't go on."

74

The girl said, direct to Agatha: "The car won't."

"Nonsense." At bay, from inside a cocoon of jersey, the woman shouted: "The thing brought you *up* this hill."

"We just made it. Something's wrong, I suppose."

"Further to that," the girl scornfully added, "we're out of petrol—all but."

"Push off; coast down—there's a pump at the bottom, in the village!"

"So we saw. But the thing is, petrol costs money."

"Well, what would you expect?"

The girl's and the youth's eyes met. He went on, this time a shade more heavily: "The thing is, we seem to be out of money."

"One-and-seven between us," the girl said proudly.

"More might come, I suppose. Someone might probably send some—that was, *if* we had an address."

"Meanwhile—for heaven's sake—what did you expect?"

"Simon had said his aunt would provide a base."

"Let us hope she may," said Agatha. "I cannot. If I could, I still don't see why I should. I'm sorry, but this has been your mistake. It's lucky for you I'm not more disagreeable than I am. Anyway, my house is completely full, and will be fuller to-morrow. I have no room for you."

"What's that, then?" asked the girl, pointing to the uninhabited wing.

"Rats and bats. Ruinous. No—impossible!"

The Art
of Bergotte

THE NAME Bergotte made me jump like the sound of
a revolver fired at me point-blank, but instinctively, for
appearance's sake, I bowed; there, straight in front of
me, as by one of those conjurors whom we see standing whole and unharmed, in their frock coats, in the
smoke of a pistol shot out of which a pigeon has just
fluttered, my salute was returned by a young common
little thick-set peering person, with a red nose curled
like a snail-shell and a black tuft on his chin. I was
cruelly disappointed, for what had just vanished in the
dust of the explosion was not only the feeble old man,
of whom no vestige now remained; there was also the
beauty of an immense work which I had contrived to
enshrine in the frail and hallowed organism that I had
constructed, but for which no room was to be found in
the squat figure, packed tight with blood-vessels, bones,
muscles, sinews, of the little man with the snub nose
and black beard who stood before me. . . . The nose
and beard were . . . the more aggravating in that,
while forcing me to reconstruct entirely the personage
of Bergotte, they seemed further to imply, to produce,
to secrete incessantly a certain quality of mind, alert
and self-satisfied, which was not in the picture, for
such a mind had no connection whatever with the sort
of intelligence that was diffused throughout those
books . . . which were permeated by a gentle and
godlike wisdom.

CONFRONTATION BY Bergotte in actuality was a dual shock. Apart from what he was like, that he should be *there* unnerved the Narrator; to whom not a hint had been dropped that the novelist was, or was to be, in the room, anywhere in the mêlée of sixteen guests at Mme. Swann's overpowering luncheon party. ("Just a few people," she had informed the youth, an enamoured contemporary of her daughter's, were to be coming.) That Bergotte, intimate with the Swanns, was known to frequent their voluptuous Paris drawing-room, with its white fur rugs, perpetual bowls of violets and many lamps (lit even in daylight), had for his worshipper, from the start, doubled the glamour of this exotic family, with its ambiguous past. By them, his Bergotte-obsession had been benevolently taken into account; today, they had staged for him a supreme surprise. The illustrious man, briefed to meet the occasion, was at the ready, the juvenile totally unprepared— that he rallied from this therefore shattering meeting was to his credit. In addition, this was his first sortie into what for all he was then to know was the *beau monde.* Due to Mme. Swann's passion for entertaining in what she conceived as being the English manner, her luncheon party was dotted with strange rites, possible pitfalls—a mystery envelope slipped to one on arrival, a carnation recumbent on one side of one's plate; on the other "a smaller plate heaped with some blackish substance which I did not then know to be caviare. I was ignorant of what was to be done with it but firmly determined not to let it enter my mouth." Thanks to the *placement,* one sat within earshot of Bergotte.

Adolescent disillusionments are many, inevitable, classic subjects for comedy. But today was a major occasion, like it or not. Of the confrontations in which *À la Recherche du temps perdu* abounds, all are dramatic, most are, when later looked back upon, to be seen as historic. All are fateful, most occur without warning. The Bergotte-Narrator confrontation was to differ from others, in this peculiarity: it led on to what became almost nothing. It marked an end, rather than a beginning. Itself a climax, if only in view of the height of the expectations it flattened, it remained the one, only climax in a relationship otherwise anticlimactic, patchy, uninspirational—a relationship haunted by what it should have been, of which the most to be said was that, throughout the years, it succeeded in never quite petering out. Nothing much came of any subsequent meeting.

Bergotte the man's obnoxious, trite, meaty physical personality had at least impacted: time and familiarity were to neutralise even that. He dematerialised, leaving only a name. Disconnected from him as a being, the books remained.

BUT A MAGNIFIED Bergotte exists on another plane. There, he is one of a triumvirate, the three artists dominant in *À la Recherche du temps perdu*. He, Elstir, Vinteuil—Writer, Painter, Composer—are ever-present in the resounding novel, few of whose major passages are uninfluenced by at least one of them. Together, they confirm the Narrator's statement: "The only truth of life is in art." Shown, also, to have acted on the characters' destinies, they are thereby precipitants of the plot: akin, in their way, to The Three Fates. Never, one may remark, is Bergotte granted quite the stature of Elstir, or of the dead Vinteuil. Those two retain an ascendancy. Their achievements expand, his reaches a limit. In *his* art, is the limit inherent? As an art, is writing subsidiary? Bergotte once totally had commanded the boy at Combray, who had yet to behold painting and hear music.

First-comer, the novelist ploughed into virgin soil.

BERGOTTE, then only known to a few readers, who composed a sort of eclectic secret society, had been recommended by the flamboyant Bloch, an *avant-garde* comrade of the Narrator's. Bloch's subsequent banishment from the Combray household, on account of one of his more ghastly remarks, did not, happily, bring about a ban on the author he had sponsored—unhindered, the boy out there in the garden read on and on:

For the first few days, like a tune which will be running in one's head and maddening one soon enough, but of which one has not for the moment "got hold," the things I was to love so passionately in Bergotte's style had not yet caught my eye. I could not, it was true, lay down the novel of his which I was reading, but I fancied that I was interested in the story alone. . . . Then I observed the rare, almost archaic phrases which he liked to employ at certain points, where a hidden flow of harmony, a prelude contained and concealed in the work itself, would animate and elevate his style; and it was at such points as these, too, that he would begin to speak of the "vain dream of life" of the "inexhaustible torrent of fair forms," of the "sterile splendid tortures of understanding and loving," of the "moving effigies which ennoble for all time the charming and venerable fronts of our cathedrals"; that he would then express a whole system of philosophy, new to me, by the use of marvellous imagery, to the inspiration of which I would naturally have ascribed that sound of harping which began to chime and echo in my ears. . . .

The experience deepened, was cumulative: "One of these passages of Bergotte's, the third or fourth which I had detached from the rest, filled me with a joy to which the meagre joy I had tasted in the first passion bore no comparison, a joy which I felt myself to have experienced in some innermost chamber of my soul."

Simultaneously, there were to be brought about two things one might have thought incompatible: identification with Bergotte, establishment of him as a father-figure. "It was suddenly revealed to me that my own humble existence and the Realms of Truth were less widely separated than I had supposed, that at certain points they were actually in contact; and in my new-found confidence and joy I wept upon his printed page, as in the arms of a long-lost father." Wish to exploit this ideal filial relation, to exchange views on all subjects under the sun, to confer, to be reciprocally in contact, to play, even, when need be, a consolatory role, became, during this first phase, in its Combray innocence, predominant: the father-affair proceeded apace— counteractive, in its respectable melancholy, to the former succession of psychic orgasms. "From his books," the Narrator remembers, "I had formed an impression of Bergotte as a frail and disappointed old man who had lost his children and never found any consolation. . . ." Hence, that "Sweet Singer with the silvery hair," to be exploded by a metaphorical pistol-shot in a Paris drawing-room.

This springtime of the romance with Bergotte has an appropriate, vernal, rural-lyrical setting: old small-town Combray, the grandparents' dignified house with its walled back-garden, the encircling countryside with its pliant contours, shallow and yet mysterious, opening-and-closing distances, changing lights. Past Combray slides, bridged, the Vivonne River. Spring warms on into early summer. Hawthorn foams into flower. A season for family walks—*"Which* way shall we go?"—*al fresco* coffee-drinking in the cool of the evenings, outdoor reading—on one occasion interrupted, dynamically, by Swann, country neighbour, paying one of his calls. "What are you reading?" the man says to the boy. "May I look? Why, it's Bergotte! Who has been telling you about him? . . . He is a charming creature. . . . I know him quite well; if you would like him to write a few words on the title-page of your book, I could ask him for you."

I noticed in the manner in which Swann spoke to me of Bergotte something which, to do him justice, was not peculiar to himself but was shared by all Bergotte's admirers at that time. . . . Like Swann, they would say of Bergotte: "He has a charming mind, so individual; he has a way of his own of saying things, which is a little far-fetched, but so pleasant. You never need look for his name on a title-page, you can tell his work at once." But none of them went so far as to say "He is a great writer, he has great talent." They did not even credit him with talent at all. They did not speak because they were not aware of it. We are very slow in recognising in the peculiar physiognomy of a new writer the type which is labelled "great talent" in our museum of general ideas.

As a rule, Swann does not talk about people he knows—he cannot be bothered. In any event, their names would mean little to Combray (to which, these days, he is a summer *revenant*). His consenting to talk about Bergotte to the boy in the garden is a concession *to* boyhood, to manifest hero-worship—and at that casual, vaguely effortful, random, full of thrown-away lines of which he does not compute the vital importance or foresee the effects. Why, yes, Bergotte—it transpires—dines with the Swanns every week (in Paris, that is). Nor is that all. "He is," Swann adds, "my daughter's greatest friend. They go about together, and look at old towns and cathedrals and castles." From that picture, inside a single sentence, desire springs. Gilberte is perceived to be the predestined love-object.

She has yet to be set eyes upon. Will she ever be? Doubt as to even that creates the requisite agonising romantic circumstance. The Swanns being, just now, in residence at nearby Tansonville, the country house inherited from his father, the girl-child must be somewhere within the white paling bounding the park. Effectually, she might be on another planet. Tansonville is, absolutely, forbidden territory. Swann having married his mistress, a former courtesan, Combray society ostracises the marriage. Among ladies who implacably do not visit is the Narrator's mother. Swann is still made welcome when he comes calling, for the sake of old days, and as his father's son. Mme. Swann, Combray rumour has it, meanwhile is disporting herself at Tansonville with a further lover. (This turns out to be the improbable Charlus.) Locally, she and her daughter have been never so much as glimpsed.

LEGEND HEIGHTENS the sense, or idea, that life is a novel—idea which continuous Bergotte-sessions also could have fostered in a young reader held back, so far, from life. One is subject to inevitabilities and compulsions, a sort of aesthetic pre-determination (he came to believe). In return, existence takes on shape and coherence; also, the comprehensibility of a story. Gilberte Swann, cause of her parents' marriage, had been given birth to (as the Narrator saw it) solely to play one part: hers with himself. She was someone Bergotte-begotten. She owed her first embodiment, faceless, indistinct, already tormenting, to envisagement of her beside the Silvery Singer, backed by "the charming and venerable" façade of a cathedral. Attendant nymph. Round the nymph-image accumulated erotic fancies. A passion, one might say, by association, whetted by readiness for more.

The coming face-to-face was, as it eventuated, a Bergotte masterpiece; equally, a full-scale Proustian confrontation. The afternoon shimmers with heat and colour. The Narrator, his grandfather and his father, out walking, are at less pains than usual to give Tansonville a wide berth, the Tansonville ladies being—it is understood—sightseeing at Rheims today, while Swann is in Paris. Even, one pauses by the white paling, to look through the thinning lilacs, purple and white, into the ostensibly empty park: expanses of lawn, tall trees, artificial lake. No, not a footstep to be heard anywhere, and a bird's note is sounding unduly loud, as though raised in protest against the solitude. But then the Narrator notices a straw basket lying forgotten on the grass by the side of a line whose float is bobbing in the water. (The float dips while one watches: a fish has bitten.) Betraying nothing, he hurries after his elders. Ahead of him, they have turned up a mounting field-path, flanked by the hawthorn hedge which is a further boundary of the Swann domain.

I found the whole path throbbing with the fragrance of hawthorn-blossom. The hedge resembled a series of chapels, whose walls were no longer visible under the mountains of flowers that were heaped on their altars; while, underneath, the sun cast a square of light upon the ground, as though it had shone in upon them through a window. . . . The flowers, themselves adorned, held out each its little bunch of glittering stamens. . . . [The flowers] here spread out into pools of fleshy white, like strawberry-beds in spring.

But far more festal, farther along the hedge comes one great pink hawthorn, clotted with blossom which has "precisely the colour of some edible and delicious thing." And of the thousand buds now swelling and opening, each disclosed, as it burst, "as at the bottom of a cup of pink marble, its blood-red stain. . . ." Wreathed by this glory, there is a gap

88

in the hedge. The Narrator again looks into the park. The foreground is not empty: he is transfixed.

. . . A little girl, with fair, reddish hair, who appeared to be returning from a walk, and held a trowel in her hand, was looking at us, raising towards us a face powdered with pinkish freckles. Her black eyes gleamed, and as I did not at that time know, and indeed have never since learned, how to reduce to its objective elements any strong impression, since I had not, as they say, enough "power of observation" to isolate the sense of their colour, for a long time afterwards, whenever I thought of her, the memory of those bright eyes would at once present itself to me as a vivid azure, since her complexion was fair; so much so that, perhaps if her eyes had not been quite so black—which was what struck one most forcibly on first meeting her —I would not have been, as I was, especially enamoured of their imagined blue.

I gazed at her . . .

In return—

. . . She cast a glance forward and sideways, so as to take stock of my grandfather and father, and doubtless the impression she formed of them was that we all were absurd people, for she turned away with an indifferent and contemptuous air. . . . [A moment later, however] while they, continuing to walk on without noticing her, had overtaken and passed me, she allowed her eyes to wander, over the space that lay between us, in my direction, without any particular expression, without appearing to have seen me, but with an intensity, a half-hidden smile which I was unable to interpret. . . .

"Gilberte, come along; what are you doing?" called out in a piercing tone of authority a lady in white. . . .

"BERGOTTE? A flute player," is M. de Norpois's considered verdict. The elderly diplomat, ex-Ambassador, is honouring the Narrator's family; he adorns their table. (Home life, in the capacious Paris apartment, had resumed its course a number of months ago, on return from the yearly visit to Combray.) Never has M. de Norpois dined here before—the *cuisine* is, he is to discover, excellent. His contact is with the Narrator's father, his ally on an anonymous commission. That his presence, for his hosts an event, is on his part an amiable condescension he feels, but does not allow to appear—has he not suffered himself already, even before dinner, to be not only shown but asked to pronounce on a literary effort of their son's? He did not think highly of it, and felt bound to say so.

Wish not to exploit or tire M. de Norpois causes the party to be confined to four: guest, host, hostess and the adolescent in question. All four being seated, M. de Norpois blandly trollies the conversation round to the Swanns—topic agreeable to the Narrator only. *En route,* there is a minute of royal name-dropping. "Now it is certain," he says, "that the Comte de Paris has always most graciously recognised the devotion of Swann, who is,

for that matter, a man of character, in spite of all."
And Mme. Swann? "She," the old boy declares, "is
altogether charming." The Swanns have made it.
M. de Norpois dined there the other night.

"Was there a writer of the name of Bergotte at
this dinner, sir?" I asked timidly. . . .
"Yes, Bergotte was there," replied M. de Norpois,
inclining his head courteously towards me. . . . "Do
you know him?" he went on, fastening on me that
clear gaze, the penetration of which had won the praise
of Bismarck.
"My son does not know him, but he admires his
work immensely," my mother explained.
"Good heavens!" exclaimed M. de Norpois.

No, he cannot share the lady's son's point of
view. Demolition of Bergotte begins. Flute-player;
a quite agreeable one, but there is mannerism, there
is affectation. And when all is said, there is nothing
so very great. Nowhere did one find in his enervated
writing anything that could be called construction.
Little action—but above all no range. "His books,"
points out M. de Norpois, "fail at the foundation, or
rather they have no foundation at all. At a time like
this, when the ever-increasing complexity of life
leaves one scarcely a moment for reading, when the
map of Europe has undergone radical alterations,
and is on the eve, probably, of undergoing others
more drastic still, when so many new and threaten-
ing problems arise on every side, you will allow me

to suggest that one is entitled to ask that a writer should be something else than a fine intellect which makes us forget, amid otiose and byzantine discussions of the merits of pure form, that we may be overwhelmed at any moment by a double tide of barbarians, those from without and those from within our borders. I am aware that this is a blasphemy against the sacrosanct school of what these gentlemen term Art for Art's sake, but at this period of history there are tasks more urgent than the manipulation of words in a harmonious manner."

And, aha—yes: *that* reminds M. de Norpois of that luckless "poem in prose" by the son of the house. One ought to have smelled a rat: the Bergotte influence! "You will not, of course, be surprised," he informs the youth, "when I say that there were in it none of his good qualities. . . . But there is the same fault. . . ."

"Given a few fireworks, let off prettily enough by an author, and up goes the shout of genius. Works of genius are not so common as all that! Bergotte cannot place to his credit—does not carry in his baggage, if I may use the expression—a single novel that is at all lofty. . . . But that does not exclude the fact that, with him, the work is infinitely superior to the author. . . . It would be impossible to imagine an individual more pretentious, more pompous, less fitted for human society."

Bergotte, it emerges, had blotted his copybook in Vienna.

"I was Ambassador there; he was presented to me by the Princess Metternich, came and wrote his name, and expected to be asked to the Embassy. Now, being in a foreign country as the Representative of France, to which he has after all done some honour by his writings, to a certain extent . . . I was prepared to set aside the unfavourable opinion that I hold of his private life. But he was not travelling alone, and he actually let it be understood that he was not to be invited without his companion. I trust that I am no more of a prude than most men . . . nevertheless, I must admit that there are depths of degradation to which I should hesitate to descend. . . . The Princess returned to the charge, but without success."

The writer's brazen and cynical behaviour was, we learn, rendered the more repulsive by contrast with the moral tone of his books. The Bergotte "moralising" had, in fact, bored M. de Norpois as much as anything else—it begins to appear. "Torturing scruples!" he grumbles. "Morbid remorse." His *liaison* with Mme. de Villeparisis, of long standing, has been chequered by nothing of that kind.

WHAT SORT of a novelist was Bergotte? He wrote *romans psychologiques*—but so did many: France cradled those. What made his work distinctive, singled it out? What characterised the Bergotte novels, basically—that is, allowing for changes in mood or manner, variations in density, gains or losses in vigour as time went on? Traceable continuity tends to underlie a creative career—a sensational break *may* be made with it, but one hears of no such break being made by Bergotte. Something, therefore, like a family trait or family tendency (accentuating, probably, with the years) would have strung his successive books together: what had they in common, one with another? A particular manner of seeing, and making seen? Sensuous imagery—cause, in the first place, of the Narrator's *engouement?* A palpable temperament, with its vocabulary—thanks to which, at the outset, he was commended for an "originality," a "charmingness" to which M. de Norpois's antipathy was itself a tribute?

That cannot have been all—the internal Bergotte could be unaccommodating and was formidable. Needing to carry the strain of revulsions, tensions, his style was of tougher fabric than first appeared. The Narrator's boyish reactions to it were not uninterruptedly rhapsodical; here, then there, he found himself brought up short—if unexpectedly stimulated—by "harshness": discordant interpolations, provincialisms, phrases deliberately strident and anti-melodic. The Sweet Singer revealed a quite other side. (Why this was not a warning, one might wonder.) The recalcitrance was genuine; the melancholy elsewhere suffusing the lovely prose was, though not a fake, in the nature of a by-product, which had undergone a refining process—call it a sublimation, sometimes over-aesthetic, of the morose, solitary, cancer-like melancholy of the man Bergotte.

Manifestly he was a master of his craft. *Le roman psychologique* suited him—gaunt in concept though it might be in principle, it invited stylishness, and lent itself to a *désabusé* romanticism: his. Since the break-away from sentimental precedent, new, free, so far unexploited areas were offering themselves to the artist pen. At the same time, this was not a revolution; a degree of orthodoxy was still required—which can have been no hardship to Bergotte. Plot, of a kind, or at least a promising "situation," was still *de rigueur*—of his novels' plots we are given little idea: they must have contained suspense, on whatever plane, for a Bergotte novel was difficult to put down. (Hence, no doubt, his ultimate surge into popularity.) One would not be surprised if his plots were trite: what matter?— he did not depend on them. (The manner of telling, of *showing,* was the thing.) And the same may have applied to his characterisation. His approach to character chiefly was analytical. Were his people, any of them, outstanding, magnetic, memorably disturbing? One has the impression that they were not. Not *they* were affective; what was affective was the magic of the climate in which they floated, the concentratedness of the vision pin-pointing them. As for their psychology?—they were Bergotte's creatures.

He was a visual writer. Imagery rendered his cadenced prose, above all, sensuous and concrete. The art in his novels acted upon the reader as does

95

a spectacle on an onlooker. There can have been nothing about the setting of a scene he did not know: everything came to have a magnified semblance of actuality. And actuality learned to imitate Bergotte—as when, for instance, that afternoon at Tansonville, one came to a stop at a gap in a hawthorn hedge.

How good a novelist was Bergotte? Ultimately, the judgement is left open.

WHICH OF THE NOVELISTS Proust knew, in Paris, as compatriots and contemporaries, was most nearly the origin of Bergotte? (A French novelist, it has to be, who was senior to Proust, though not necessarily by a great number of years. Was not Bergotte's unexpected youthfulness [of a gross kind] not the least of the shocks?) Once—that is, when I first read *À la Recherche du temps perdu,* in the nineteen-twenties—*I* would have said Bourget. Now, re-reading the work with particular concentration on Bergotte, I find Bourget recedes. His novels, as I recollect them, were indeed "psychological"—more drastically so, probably, than were Bergotte's—but unenhanced by the harp-soundings (or "flute-playing") which so beatifically acted on the Narrator. He concentrated on being a fashionable iconoclast. Barrès, against whose insidious *Culte du moi* trilogy, which was gaining ground, Bourget's *Le Disciple* aimed an ethical (and best-selling) blow, could seem the likelier of the two to have upheaved young

Proust, as did Bergotte the young Narrator. Barrès was an at once clear-cut and limpid stylist: an *élitist,* both in method and aim. But Proust and Barrès, in Paris, were little in contact; there existed between them nothing equivalent, even, to the *manqué* but still-persistent relationship there was between the Narrator and Bergotte. Of the gulf opened up by the Dreyfus case, they were on opposite sides. . . .

Exploratory work done on Proust and his personal world, in the last years, more and more brings forward Anatole France as a—in fact, as *the*— Bergotte candidate. France it was, it now is strongly suggested, who was the Master, the awakener of and predominant influence on creative awareness— or awareness of what it could be to be creative—in the young Proust. What France wrote inspired the early writing, and was its model. Substantially there was a France-Bergotte alikeness; snout nose, detestable little beard, thick-set physical bounciness, and, worst, lack of venerability were, in one first fell moment, to devastate Proust. The tottering idol, rather too much at home in the drawing-room in which he was first encountered, was lover *en titre* of the hostess, a distinguished *salonnière.* Of Bergotte's love life, apart from the nameless lady he arrived in Vienna with, we hear nothing till its humiliating last phases. He was said by many to be unkind to his wife; so was Anatole France. France was consistently friendly to Proust; spoke highly of

him as an emerging writer, would have been glad to
see more of him, wrote him a preface, and went out
of his way to do him other good turns. This good
will, Proust reciprocated, if temperately.

Ruskin, on the strength of stylistic influence,
keying-up effect on the Proust aesthetic and engen-
derment of the passion for cathedrals, has been
named as at least a constituent of Bergotte. As anywhere present in Bergotte, I cannot see him. One
must stop somewhere. Bergotte is a composite character: accepted? Like the otherwise very different
Saint-Loup, he has group-origin. Or call it multiple
origin. There are as many young-noblemen candidates for Saint-Loup as there are literary candidates
for Bergotte. Both integrate, miraculously, as individuals; but Saint-Loup, besides being conspicu-
ously attractive, to a degree which Bergotte con-
spicuously is not, is the more completely perceived,
the more "realized" of the two, for this reason: in
Saint-Loup there is nothing of Proust; in Bergotte
there is much. Bergotte is a stand-in, scape-goat,
whipping-boy for his creator. Hence Proust's recur-
ring, uneasy unjustness to him. Those Bergotte purple patches (worse, it is true, in English), the "torrents of fair forms," and so on, could be burlesques
of Proust's own at their early worst—how he once
had written could continue to haunt him. For a long
time, had he not laboured under the charge of "pre-
ciousness?"—*he* knew what it was to be patronised
as "charming." . . . Just as he transferred his

homosexuality to Charlus, Proust shifted on to Bergotte his literary guilt, with its nexus of ignominies, self-searchings and anxieties. Charges brought against Bergotte of being (socially) "ambitious—utterly selfish," the Narrator makes no attempt to rebut. But, it is pointed out,

those vices did not at all prove . . . that his literature was a lie and all his sensitiveness mere play-acting. . . . There may be a vice arising from supersensitiveness just as much as from the lack of it. Perhaps it is only in really vicious lives that the moral problem can arise in all its disquieting strength. And of this problem the artist finds a solution not in terms of his own personal life but of what for him is the true life, a general, a literary solution. As the great Doctors of the Church began often, without losing their virtue, by acquainting themselves with the sins of all mankind, so great artists often, while being thoroughly wicked, make use of their vices in order to arrive at a conception of the moral law which is binding upon us all.

The notion of purgation, of self-redemption, of bought-back virtue being possible for the artist by means of art recurs throughout *À la Recherche du temps perdu,* from volume to volume, with ever-accumulating force. It interlocks, for instance, with the notion of immortality, in the passage following Bergotte's death:

Permanently dead? Who shall say? . . . All we can say is that everything is arranged in this life as though we entered it carrying the burden of obligations contracted in a former life. . . . All these obligations which have not their sanction in our present life seem to belong to a different world, founded upon kindness, scrupulosity, self-sacrifice, a world entirely different from this, which we leave in order to be born into this one, before perhaps returning to the other to live once more under the sway of those unknown laws which we have obeyed because we bore their precepts in our hearts, knowing not whose hand had traced them there —those laws to which every profound work of the intellect brings us nearer and which are invisible only —and still!—to fools. So that the idea that Bergotte was not wholly and permanently dead is by no means improbable.

(*"Our birth is but a sleep and a forgetting"?* It could be that amongst the torments of the artist is this—that in his case the oblivion is not complete?)

GILBERTE, as compared to the later Albertine, comes, finally, more or less unscathed out of her involvement with the Narrator. Highly romanticisable, Gilberte was not born to be a romantic's prey. The sadistic love-tactics that were to be employed with Albertine fall flat when tried out on an immune schoolgirl—Swann's cherished only child. Gilberte, tolerantly referred to by M. de Norpois, that famous evening, as "a young person of about fourteen or fifteen," would not have been much above that age when she and the Narrator began their games in the Champs-Élysées; nor (so far as

one can make out) can he have been much more.
She gave no signs of being sexually precocious: the
wrestling-match, erotic for the Narrator, was for
Mlle. Swann, apparently, simply an agreeable
rough-and-tumble. As her family saw it, this was a
boy-and-girl affair—the unseriousness of it in their
eyes probably diminished it in hers. She tended to
be more off-hand, capricious or sullen with the Narrator when her parents were there. Only many years
afterwards, when it had ceased to matter, was he to
learn that still waters had run deep—Gilberte (in a
womanhood made unhappy by marriage to the un-
faithful Saint-Loup) gives the Narrator her version
of their encounter at Tansonville. On seeing him,
she instantly had desired him. (Hence the equivocal
smile on the childish face, and the sliding glance.)

It was because of Bergotte that he had fallen
in love with her, he tells her. That, one may take it,
she knew. They had talked, talked, talked about
Bergotte—at the beginning. Bored or piqued by a
little too much Bergotte, did Gilberte then set about
to displace him? She did so; that she should was,
after all, in the course of nature. Beside the physical
girl, the ethereal Singer had not a chance—that
was, as an obsession. The unattainability of Gilberte—not lessened, indeed made more to be felt by
knowing her, together with not knowing if, and if
so by what means, he could know her better—
caused her to drain off from the Narrator any fac-
ulty for any kind of desire other than his for her.

The paradox of romantic love—that what one possesses, one can no longer desire—was at work. Did he not "possess" (through its entering into him, he into it) Bergotte's art? So now he thought of it less. Yet it continued to play a part, to remain in association with what was happening. Gilberte, as promised, brings the Narrator a rare pamphlet of Bergotte's. This is a moment: "As for Bergotte, that infinitely wise, almost divine old man . . . now it was for Gilberte's sake, chiefly, that I loved him. With as much pleasure as the pages he had written about Racine, I studied the wrapper, folded under great seals of white wax and tied with billows of pink ribbon, in which she had brought those pages to me." The seals, the ribbon, bespoke "the mysterious charm of Gilberte's life."

At the start, meetings are in the Champs-Élysées—in the playground glade where they first spoke to each other—only. Suspense attends on them: sometimes for days together she fails to appear. Where is she: at home? That home, is he ever, or never, to enter? That he does do so—that not only Swann but his wife (who well might, even splendidly here in Paris, have repaid some of the snubs she had had from Combray) makes him welcome, shows for him such an affection that it amounts to, virtually, adopting him—leads up, as we are to know, to the luncheon party at which his main desire (as they saw it) was to be gratified.

.   .   .

THAT THE NARRATOR sits in earshot of Bergotte
gives Proust occasion to stress the social cynicism,
the up-thrusting provincialism, yet the eventual—it
could be involuntary—tunings-in of the true artist.
Bergotte's conversation, as listened-in to, goes
through changes of gear. One understands only too
well, at first, the impression formed by M. de
Norpois; Bergotte had indeed a peculiar "organ."
Or the voice is as though issuing "from behind a
mask." It was not till later on that:

> I discovered an exact correspondence with the
> parts of his books in which his form became so poetic
> and so musical. At those points, he could see in what
> he was saying a plastic beauty independent of whatever
> his sentences might mean, and as human speech reflects
> the human soul, though without expressing it as does
> literary style, Bergotte appeared almost to be talking
> nonsense. . . .
> Certain peculiarities of elocution, faint traces of
> which were to be found in Bergotte's conversation,
> were not exclusively his own; for when, later on, I
> came to know his brothers and sisters, I found these
> peculiarities much more accentuated in their speech.
> . . . Those young Bergottes—the future writer and
> his brothers and sisters—were doubtless in no way
> superior, far from it, to other young people, more
> refined, more intellectual than themselves, who found
> the Bergottes rather "loud."

But, "men who produce works of genius are not
those who live in the most delicate atmosphere, but

those who have had the power . . . to make use of
their personality as a mirror, in such a way that
their life, however unimportant it may be, is reflected by it, genius consisting in the reflective
power of the writer and not in the intrinsic quality
of the scene reflected."

Before the party breaks up, the Narrator has
not only moved in upon, but has had—he learns—
a heady success with Bergotte. "You can't think
how delighted I am," Gilberte whispers into his ear,
"because you have made a conquest of my great
friend. He's been telling Mamma that he found you
extremely intelligent." He and Bergotte leave the
party together: in the carriage they talk about
health—the Narrator's, defective—then, *à propos*,
doctors.

"I'll tell you who does need a good doctor, and
that is our friend Swann," said Bergotte. And, on my
asking whether he was ill, "Well, don't you see, he's
typical of a man who has married a whore, and has to
swallow a hundred serpents every day, from women
who refuse to meet his wife, or men who were there
before him. You can see them in his mouth, writh-
ing. . . ." The malice with which Bergotte spoke thus
to a stranger of the friends in whose house he had
been so long received as a welcome guest was as new
to me as the almost amorous tone which, in that house,
he had constantly been adopting to speak to them.

CRUELTY INFESTS, as might a malevolent fever a
swamp or jungle, the universe of *À la Recherche du*

temps perdu—the marvel is that it does not poison it wholly: life, with its perennial innocence, survives. The characters have an astonishing resilience, a fool-hardy, desperado quality which gives them panache: almost all of them are at bay. Bergotte, for instance, knows all there dares to be known about the snake-pit of literary politics; the days of his high reputation are to be numbered (as are, indeed, those of his life on earth). Neither he nor that other whipping-boy, Charlus, can be made chargeable with the crime that is central in the vast novel: a cannibalistic romanticism. That, the Narrator alone carries the onus of—*unless* Proust identifies with the Narrator. How far did Proust identify with the Narrator; how far objectify (and thereby disclaim) him? The destruction of Albertine, by means of a long-drawn-out demoralisation, is horrible. There had been gleams of virtue, of tenderness, of aspiration to harmony in the love for Gilberte: few remained in the love meted out to Albertine. There was sporadic remorse—the "morbid remorse" of Bergotte?; there was never pity. Albertine, after her flight and following death, had to be exorcised—and at length was.

BERGOTTE'S WRITING lost attraction for the Narrator when, with time, it became easy to read:

His sentences stood out as clearly before my eyes as my own thought, the furniture in my room and the

carriages in the streets. . . . But a new writer had recently begun to publish work in which the relations
between things were so different from anything that
connected them for me that I could understand hardly
anything of what he wrote. . . . I felt, nevertheless,
for the new writer the admiration which an awkward
boy who never receives any marks for gymnastics feels
when he watches another more nimble. And from then
on I felt less admiration for Bergotte, whose limpidity
began to strike me as insufficient.

Ironically, a series of visits received from Bergotte,
at this time, for the Narrator came several years too
late. However, they, or at least the idea of them,
gave comfort to his father and mother, and were
felt to honour his grandmother, who, in the family
apartment, now lay dying.

Here, in another room, sat the speechless
Bergotte, day after day, for hours on end—a sick
man. Fame has terribly overtaken him.

The general rule is, no doubt, that only after his
death does a writer become famous. But it was while
he still lived, and during his slow progress towards a
death that he had not yet reached, that this writer was
able to watch the progress of his works towards Re-
nown. A dead writer can at least be illustrious without
any strain on himself. . . . He [Bergotte] existed, still,
sufficiently to suffer from the tumult. . . .
The bulk of his thought had long since passed
from his brain into his books. He had grown thin, as
though they had been extracted from him in surgical
operations. . . . He led the vegetative life of a conva-

lescent, of a woman after childbirth; his fine eyes remained motionless, vaguely dazed, like the eyes of a
man who lies on the sea shore and in a vague daydream sees only each little breaking wave.

Now, "the passion for Bergotte's works was
unbounded." Alone in an inclement apartment,
sometimes, when chilly, with a grubby tartan rug
over his knees, he was apologetic when he received
company—discouraged, his visitors dwindled to almost none. Doctors contradicted each other across
him. He appears miserly; actually, much of the new
money has been bestowed on various derelict little
girls he had hired, in the last years, to come in and
sleep with him, having come to the conclusion that
it is less humiliating to buy love than to fail to win
it. "What I have squandered, all the same!" he reflected sometimes. He went out only out of fear of
contracting the habit of staying in—and then, only
to houses in which he need not speak. (He now had
a speech-obstruction.)

There are two instances in *À la Recherche du
temps perdu* of the Narrator's stepping clear of the
"I" and entering the experience of another person.
One is when he "becomes" Swann, for the duration
of Swann's love-affair with Odette, the other when
he "becomes" Bergotte, for the minutes before and
at the moment of Bergotte's death. Bergotte had
been ordered to rest. But on learning that morning,
from something said by a critic, that Vermeer's

View of Delft, lent by the gallery at The Hague, was on view in Paris, he ate a few potatoes, left the house and went to the exhibition. On the stairs up to it he had an attack of giddiness. Making his way through the rooms, he passed Dutch pictures which struck him as stiff, futile and artificial. At last he came to the Vermeer, which he had imagined he knew by heart, which he remembered as more striking, more different, than anything else he knew. And so it was. This time, thanks to the critic, he remarked for the first time some small blue figures. There, too, more precious than ever in substance, was the tiny patch of yellow wall. His giddiness increased: "He fixed his eyes, like a child upon a yellow butterfly which it is trying to catch, upon the precious little patch of wall."

"That is how I ought to have written," he said. "My last books are too dry, I ought to have gone over them with several coats of paint, made my language exquisite in itself, like this little patch of yellow wall." Meanwhile, he was not unconscious of the gravity of his condition. In a celestial balance there appeared to him, upon one of its scales, his own life, while the other contained the little patch of wall so beautifully painted in yellow. He felt that he had rashly surrendered the former for the latter. "All the same," he said to himself, "I have no wish to provide the 'feature' of this exhibition for the evening papers."

He repeated to himself: "Little patch of yellow wall, with a sloping roof, little patch of yellow wall."

Sinking on to a divan, he felt better. . . . "It's

just an ordinary indigestion from those potatoes; they weren't cooked properly." A fresh attack beat him down; he rolled from the divan to the floor. . . . He was dead. They buried him, but all through the night of mourning, in the lighted windows, his books arranged three by three kept watch like angels with outspread wings and seemed, for him who was no more, the symbol of his resurrection.

Proust while dying thought about Bergotte's death—there was something, he made known, that he wanted to add.

Nativity Play

[*The production of this play has its own small, but perhaps significant, place in history. When it was presented in the Protestant Cathedral in Londonderry, that town saddened by much bitterness and bloodshed, it was, so Elizabeth's friend Derek Hill, who acted as one of the Narrators, believes, the first ecumenical event ever to be held there—Anglicans, Presbyterians, and Catholics all taking part and Catholics for the first time forming part of the congregation. Elizabeth had been anxious that such a unity of response should be manifest and it must have caused her not only pleasure but, I hope, pride.* S.C.B.]

PROLOGUE TO ACT I

(The Curtain has not yet risen)

Open: *"Hallelujah" Chorus—with trumpets.*
Followed by *Carol: "In Dulci Jubilo."*

1ST NARRATOR *(a woman)*:
    A Star rose
    In the East

2ND NARRATOR:
    Over a great tract
    —Here, peopled with cities
    —There, inhuman and empty as the moon,
    Boundless,
    Cleft
    By precipitous gorges
    Run through by rivers,
    Whose gentler valleys
    Rustle with green young trees
    Making sweet the air . . .
    But parched are the deserts
    And their sands.
    And harsh soar the mountains
    —Their rocks are castles,
    Their castles rocks.
    Eagles circle over them.

1ST NARRATOR:

Since Man began,
Kings have reigned in these strongholds
On those cities,
Merciless,
Waging wars. . . .
Bones come to nothing
Blow about in the dust
And Nature is not less terrible than Man.

2ND NARRATOR:

Winds shriek round the bitten hills,
In the icy winter,
And numb the plains.
The hills are, within,
Hollow with caves
In whose cold was shelter
For many tribes.
Summer, its sun smiting like a sword,
Is to be feared.

1ST NARRATOR:

Yet there also are lakes,
And fishermen,
Paths round fields' edges,
Shaded gardens
And singing birds,
Sheep cropping the grass on the uplands,
And shepherds guarding them.

2ND NARRATOR:

Over all this,
God—
Maker of All—
Stretched His hand out
—Of old.

Setting free his people,
Sending them out of Egypt,
Across the desert,
Down the sides of the mountains,
Across Jordan,
Into the Promised Land.

1ST NARRATOR:
And in that land,
There—still—was a Promise
To be fulfilled.
The Star stood in the sky
Over that land.

(*Pause*)

2ND NARRATOR:
In the year of the Star,
In the East,
There were three watchers:
Star-gazers.
Three Wise Men—
Kings, we are told.

1ST NARRATOR:
They made no wars,
We may be sure.
Dedicated to learning,
They sought peace. . . .
Far apart
The kingdoms beneath their serene reign.
Each of them,
In the solitude of his wisdom,
Scanned the skies, nightly,
In silence, year after year
—Then, bent his head over his study table.

2ND NARRATOR:
> Yet these three
> Knew of each other's minds. . . .
> How did they meet,
> And when?
> Perhaps, once a year?

1ST NARRATOR:
> Once a year,
> By night,
> In a tent set up
> Somewhere
> In the no-man's-land of the desert?

The Curtain Rises

ACT I

The Three Kings

SCENE: *A tent in the desert.*
TIME: *Night, in spring.*
The tent is large, and draped in a royal manner. In the centre of the stage, a little to the back, is a throne-like chair. Near it, a table on which is a crystal-gazer's globe; and the rest of the table is strewn with parchments.

The light of a lamp falls on the parchments. Elsewhere, the tent is softly though richly lit. To the L. and R. are divans, or cushions stacked up to form seats. To the L. and R. are entrances.

When the CURTAIN rises, 1st King (whose tent this is) stands gazing fixedly outward and upward at the starry sky, through the entrance-aperture L.

1ST KING:

    How bright they are,
    And how still they seem.
    Countless,
    Burning the sky up with their white fire.
    Burning. . . ?
    A flame trembles, a star does not.

    (*Pause*)

    O you stars, stars, stars,
    Unpitying eyes, eyes, eyes,
    Inexorable in your knowing and fixed gaze,
    Do you behold me, as I you?

(The 1st King, making a great gesture, covers his eyes with the back of his hand. He then turns away from the door and looks round the tent. He listens intently.)

Is that you, my friends?
My fellow-Kings?
My Philosopher-brothers?
From the ends of the earth,
Through the unechoing silences of the desert,
Your two great caravans, converging—
Just now, was *that* what I heard?
Is it you that I hear?

(He again listens, then gives a satisfied sigh.)

Yes . . .

Enter R. a young Attendant. He salutes, then ushers in 2nd King. Exit Attendant.
(The 1st and 2nd Kings salute one another with low obeisances.)

2ND KING:
Another year has gone by.

1ST KING:
Another year has gone by.

(They look at each other.)

2ND KING:
Your stature is no less.

1ST KING:
Nor is yours, my friend.

(The 2nd King looks eagerly at the parchments on the tables. He stretches out a hand, as though to touch them, but then withdraws the hand.)

118

2ND KING:
> You have travelled in mind,
> How far?
> Since we last met, what have your thoughts been?
> Your conquest? Your discoveries?
> What have you to show me?

1ST KING (*in a voice of stone*):
> I have come to a standstill.

2ND KING (*startled*):
> *I* have come to a standstill.

1ST KING:
> What is this threshold we cannot cross?
>
> (*Tramping feet*)
> (*Trumpet call*)
> (*He breaks off, turns his head, listens.*)
>
> Here—I think?—comes Kaspar.

2ND KING:
> How has he fared—I wonder?
>
> (*The 1st and 2nd Kings compose themselves into formal attitudes of expectation, looking towards the entrance L.*)
> *Enter L. Attendant. He salutes, then ushers in 3rd King. Exit Attendant.*
> (*The 3rd King salutes the 1st and 2nd Kings with low obeisances. They return the obeisances.*)

3RD KING:
> Had I had wings,
> I would have been with you before now.
> Never has a year gone by more slowly,
> Never has the path of my own mind
> Been more cold and lonely.

And it has led me where?
To the edge of a gulf.

(*He stretches his hands out to the two others.*)

I have been sorely in need of you,
My two friends,
O my brothers in wisdom,
Be now my elders?
Speak to me,
Tell me,
Show me a guiding light!

1ST KING (*to 3rd King*):
You are weary after the journey?
       (*to 2nd King*):
You must be weary?

1ST KING (*to both*):
Be seated.

(*He indicates the throne-chair.*)

Which of you, my King-brothers,
Will take the throne?

2ND KING (*shaking his head*):
Not I.

(*He seats himself on a divan R.*)

3RD KING (*shaking his head*):
Nor I.

(*He seats himself on a divan L.*)

1ST KING (*looking at the throne, then making a gesture
of dissension*):

For me? No,
Above all, for me—no!

(*He speaks to the throne-chair.*)

Throne, you must wait.
Wait.

(*Folding his arms, he remains standing.*)

Alone, I have read the heavens,
To a point where I can no longer see.
What more have the stars to say to us—*what
   more?*
Their blaze is a mystery.
Seeming immovable—as might the diamonds
   set into my crown.
Or into yours—or into yours, my friends—
They are moving.
They are the movers; we are the watchers,
On our apart tower-tops.
"The Order of the Heavens," we say, bowing to it,
For we are wise men.
But . . . under *Whose* order are the heavens?
In this last year, I have come to ask myself that.
And my mind stumbled.
One cannot worship an Order in itself.
In whose mind are these millions of
   burning thoughts?
What is the Intention?

2ND KING:
   I have asked myself that.

3RD KING:
   And I. I await the answer.
   What is the answer?

1ST KING (*speaking diffidently and slowly*):

Suppose . . .

(*He turns and goes to the door L. and again stares outward and upward at the sky.*)
Suppose that the scintillating and
   boundless heavens,
Together with this our familiar earth,
Are one single throne,
Waiting?

2ND KING:
   For whom?

1ST KING:
   A king of Kings?
   A king of Heaven and Earth?

3RD KING:
   Waiting . . .
   For how long?
   How long *more?*

1ST KING:
   This is spring.
   All springs are new, but this is like no other!
   Rivers are rushing through the land as
      never before.
   The wind's breath carries a sweetness
   More disturbing
   Than ever before.
   The awakening birds
   Sing such a song, this year, as we never knew.
   The flowers are brighter; scarlet and
      sky-blue carpets
   Are flung out over the stony hills,
   In expectation of Whose feet?
   Who is coming?
   Who is to be the Newcomer?

(*Pause*)

As for the stars . . .
Are *they* not capable of amazement?
Tonight, while I was waiting for you,
Their gaze smote me with its alert brilliance.
What has alerted the stars?
Planets and satellites, what do *they* await?

2ND KING:
    One more?
    Some unforeseeable Other, yet to rise?

3RD KING (*indicating the crystal globe*):
    What says our crystal?
    Locked in its clouded, dark sphere, it holds
        the future.
    Shall I look?
    Dare I see?

2ND KING:
    Dare to look.

1ST KING:
    Try to see.

   (*3rd King bends over the crystal and stares into it.*)

3RD KING (*at last*):
    Nothing.

2ND KING (*incredulous*):
    Nothing?
    What is the matter with the crystal?

   (*2nd King takes 3rd King's place at the crystal, and
stares into it.*)

123

2ND KING (*at last*):
Nothing . . .
Unfriendly crystal! (*He smites the crystal.*)
What are you withholding?
Never, never before have you not spoken!
Now,
What you know, you veil,
You veil from our seeing—
What *is* this what you know?

1ST KING:
Patience, my friend!

(*He takes 2nd King's place at the crystal but no more than glances into it.*)

Something confounds the crystal,
Confounds magic.

(*He puts the crystal aside.*)

Let us turn
To learning.

(*He indicates the many scrolls on the table, picks up one, and frowningly studies it.*)

Here let us search . . .

(*The 2nd and 3rd Kings pick scrolls from the table, and do likewise. They pass the scrolls from hand to hand, comparing them.*)

2ND KING:
Even if we search in vain?

1ST KING:
Even if we search in vain . . .

3RD KING:
We Three,
Who are come to a standstill?

124

1ST KING (*bowing his head*):

> Yes.
> Here we enter the country of humility.
> All this—

> (*He passes his hand over the writing on a parchment.*)

> All this has been written,
> Yet—still—where are we?
> Always, forever, only upon the verges,
> Of the vastness of knowledge.

> (*He puts the scroll down.*)

2ND KING (*putting his scroll down*):
> Yet,
> How if a Voice spoke?

3RD KING (*putting his scroll down*):
> If a Sign came?
> If a Light shone?

> (*The three Kings look at each other.*)
> (*Pause*)
> (*The 1st King raises his arms, in supplication, to the unseen sky above the top of the tent.*)

1ST KING:

> O Star,
> O Unknown,
> O Star the heavens await,
> Wherever Thou art,
> Whatever Thou be,
> Rise!
> Guide us!
> Show us the way,
> Lighten our darkness!

Curtain

125

PROLOGUE TO ACT II

Toccata and Fugue in D Minor—Bach
*Carol: "As Joseph Went A-Walking." Choir and
organ.*

2ND NARRATOR:
Crossing a great green plain
You perceive mountains.
High among those sits Nazareth,
A small town,
Friendly little white houses
Set about with cypresses, fig-trees, olives,
And airy fields.

1ST NARRATOR:
In that beautiful spring
It was quiet, sunny,
Unknown to fame.
Who, dwelling in Nazareth, could wish to be more
Or other
Than what they were?
Neighbours were neighbours;
Children grew up together.

2ND NARRATOR:
Seldom did a stranger pass this way;
Nazareth was far from the world's thoughts.

1ST NARRATOR:
Nazareth had one fountain,

To which, in the shining hour before sunset,
Women and girls went out,
To bring home water . . .
Among them, Mary.

2ND NARRATOR:
Here lived Mary.

1ST NARRATOR:
The young Mary,
Espoused to Joseph, the carpenter. . . .
Life lay ahead of Mary,
Foreseeable,
Settled and sure and simple,
Until the Angel came,
That day.

2ND NARRATOR:
That day,
Can it have dawned on Mary like *any* spring day.
Like any other?

1ST NARRATOR:
Could such a day
Have dawned on Mary like any other?

(*Pause*)

Was the day spent
—As though it *were* any other—
In her home, at her tasks,
With her friends?
Or
Did she go out,
Alone to be alone,
Not knowing where she went,
Or for what cause,

Or for how long?
Wondering?

2ND NARRATOR:
Telling no one?

1ST NARRATOR:
Shall we think,
That was so?

2ND NARRATOR:
It could have been so.

1ST NARRATOR:
Suppose it were so.
See—

The Curtain Rises

In her home,
Here are friends of Mary's,
Other Nazareth girls
Who have come in,
As girls do, when they are friends, often.
They are waiting for her,
Waiting for Mary,
Puzzled . . .

ACT II

The Annunciation

SCENE: *Mary's home, in Nazareth.*
TIME: *A spring evening, before sunset.*
A simple room, white-walled and full of light. In the centre-back is an archway, behind which hangs a curtain. There are entrances L. and R.

To the R. of the stage, forward, is a weaving-frame with a low stool. To the L. is a group of pieces of pottery, rough but shapely—some bowls, a water-pot (such as is carried on the head) and one small beaker.

When the CURTAIN rises, 1st Young Girl is on-stage. Seated in front of the weaving-frame, she has an air of waiting. To fill in time she is, somewhat idly and inexpertly, working the shuttle. Enter 2nd Young Girl. She carries some scarlet anemones, such as grow in the fields.

2ND YOUNG GIRL (*looking round room*):
Where's Mary?

1ST GIRL:
That's what *I* wonder!

2ND GIRL:
Gone to the well, d'you think?

1ST GIRL:
No; because

(*pointing*)

There's her water-pot.

2ND GIRL (*looking into the water-pot*):
And full, too.

(*Reflects*)

She was out early.

(*2nd Girl dips the beaker into the water-pot and, having thus filled it, sets the anemones in it.*)
(*1st Girl returns to idling with the shuttle of the weaving-frame.*)

2ND GIRL (*observing 1st Girl*):
Ought you to be tampering with her work?

1ST GIRL:
I'm doing no harm to it.
And she'd never forbid me;
She's very gentle.

2ND GIRL:
Yes.

(*Pause*)

What is it sets her apart,
From you and me?
It's not pride—no,
In all her speaking and doing
She's gentle,
She's the gentlest among us. . . .
Is it that look she wears?
Her look is her beauty—wouldn't you say?

1ST GIRL (*nodding*):
I would.

2ND GIRL:
Or is it her silence, sometimes?
Is it her thoughts?
You and I speak out; we don't think, much.
But Mary—all of a sudden she's miles away!

1ST GIRL:

>Who's to say what it is?
>We could never follow her.

>*(She starts back from the weaving-frame with an expression of dismay.)*

>Ah, look at me now!
>I've got in a muddle.
>You're right, I shouldn't be tampering.
>I'm the idle one!

>*(Laughs)*

>Though you are as bad,
>With your flower-picking!
>Ah, well, we're young, so there's time enough,
>But we're young still,
>You and I and she,
>You and I and Mary.

>*(She rises, pauses, looks round, puzzled.)*

>All the same, it's funny;
>It's not like her.
>Is it?
>I mean, this evening
>—To be going away from her home
>With never a word. . . .
>I don't understand—
>Has she forgotten, would you say?

2ND GIRL:

>Would she ever?
>This was to be *our* evening,
>The first of spring.
>The three of us were to be going out
>Together. Walking about the fields

131

Till the sun sets. As we do every spring,
Since first we were children.
Hand in hand,
Singing our same songs—

1ST GIRL:
That we love to sing.

2ND GIRL:
But she's gone without us?

(*The two girls look at each other, askance. A sound is heard from off-stage L.*)

1ST GIRL (*holding her hand up*):
Hsssst!

(*Both girls look to L. expectantly.*)

2ND GIRL:
That's not her hand on the latch.
That's not her step.

Joseph's voice (*calling from off-stage*):

Mary?

1ST GIRL:
That's Joseph.

2ND GIRL:
It is,
It's Joseph.

Enter Joseph. (*A man of about thirty, upright, strong-looking and gentle, of open countenance. He wears the rough, stripped-down clothes of a carpenter straight from work.*)

1ST GIRL (*to Joseph*):
Are you looking for Mary?

JOSEPH (*looking about him*):
Where's she gone, do you know?

(*Both girls shake their heads.*)

2ND GIRL:
We couldn't tell you.

1ST GIRL:
Was there anything you wanted?

JOSEPH:
Only to set eyes on her,
And to tell her—it's been a great day,
Today. A long, great day
—I'm building our house!

(*Stretching his arms, tired but happy.*)

I've been working like ten men.

1ST GIRL:
That must be a wonderful thing—

2ND GIRL:
Building your home!

JOSEPH:
Yes.
It's only the shape of the thing, still;
It's only begun.
The walls are only that high.

(*He measures low, with his hand.*)

But they're strong already.
The rest of it's still in the air.
But isn't the air sweet today?

133

Isn't the air lovely and full of promise,
The air of spring?
Today I laid the threshold-stone
For our door. And I measured the hearth out—
I'll lay *that* tomorrow.
Then—wait till I have the roof on!

(*He steps back and looks upward, as though seeing it.*)

Already I'm seeing the days to come,
And the years to be
Our one life, under the one roof. . . .
I ask no more.

1ST GIRL:
Isn't that a wonderful thing?

2ND GIRL:
To ask no more!

JOSEPH:
They speak of Destiny,
And how that can single a man out,
Driving him forth on dark, bitter journeys
Into the far-away,
Forcing him up into high and terrible places,
Into the stare of the world.
They say
That when Destiny's coming your way,
You hear its footfalls.
Ah, *I* should never care to hear those footfalls!
And nor shall I.
Destiny's after the Great.
It will pass me by,
Me and Mary,

The simple ones, here in this quiet place,
Asking no more.

(*Change of tone; suddenly becoming sad.*)

But now the sun's going down,
The shadows grow longer.
I left my work.
I wanted a word with her,
Wanted to say to her how the day has gone.
And I thought,
Maybe, she'd give me a glass of water.

2ND GIRL:
Will I give you a glass of water?

(*She takes the anemones from the beaker, scattering them carelessly on the floor. She empties the beaker, rinses the beaker, brings it out refilled. She brings it to Joseph.*)
(*He drinks, though listlessly. Handing the beaker back, he sees the anemones on the floor.*)

JOSEPH:
That's no way to treat Mary's flowers!

2ND GIRL (*quickly*):
I brought them in.

JOSEPH:
All the same,
They're innocent, helpless things.
Why not leave them be?
They had only a day.

1ST GIRL:
She brought them for Mary.

JOSEPH:
You did?
They're pretty enough.

135

But not Mary's colour;
Her colour's blue
—Sky-blue in the morning,
Night-blue at night,
Blue. . . .

(*He looks again at the anemones.*)

I don't care to see these,
Lying. They're like spilled blood.
Gather them up.

(*Pause*)

Well, I'll be going.

2ND GIRL (*not picking up the anemones*):
Looking for her?

1ST GIRL:
She might be far off, still;
Away out over the country
—You never know.

JOSEPH:
I know the last of the day's
Still bright. The hills are golden.
Wherever she may be,
Or may be going,
The sun will stay in the heavens
To shine on Mary.
—Tell her I was looking for her, if you *see* her.

(*He salutes both girls, fraternally.*)
*Exit Joseph, L. The two girls look across at each
other, as though to speak. But there is a pause until—*

1ST GIRL (*reaching out her hand to 2nd Girl*):
Let's us two go out, shall we?
Before the sunset?

2ND GIRL:
Us two only?

1ST GIRL (*looking round room sadly*):
Next year, she'll be gone from us
In any event.
Next spring, there'll *be* only us two left,
Singing in the fields.

2ND GIRL:
Together,
Singing the same songs,
As we always sang?

(*2nd Girl takes 1st Girl's outstretched hand. They
go out together.*) Exit 1st Girl and 2nd Girl, R.

*The STAGE, which has been very slightly darkening,
remains empty. Pause—which should be marked and of
some length. Then—*

1ST NARRATOR (*voice as though taking up where it had
left off*):
A virgin espoused
To a man whose name was Joseph,
Of the House of David;
And the virgin's name was
Mary.

*Enter Mary, L. She comes in slowly, as far as the
centre of the stage. She looks, though as without seeing
them, at the scattered anemones. Then, turns and looks
(hardly more seeingly) at her weaving-frame with the
stool pushed back from it. She seats herself at the frame*

137

and puts out a hand, as though in a dream, to touch the
shuttle. But she does not.

    Slowly, the curtain hanging in the archway begins to
fill up with light. A supernatural brightness dissolves the
curtain. As this happens, Mary rises, hand to her breast.
She advances towards (or seems, rather, drawn towards)
the archway. At its foot, she falls on her knees, though still
looking up. The Angel appears in the archway.

2ND NARRATOR:

    And the Angel came in unto her,
    And said,
    "Hail, thou that are highly favoured,
    The Lord is with thee;
    Blessed art thou among women."

    (*Mary shrinks back as she kneels. She covers her*
eyes.)

    And when she saw him she was troubled at
        his saying,
    And cast in her mind, what manner of
        salutation this should be?
    And the angel said unto her,
    "Fear not,
    Mary,
    For thou has found favour with God.
    And, behold—
    Thou shalt conceive in thy womb, and
        bring forth
    A son,
    And shall call his name
    JESUS.
    He shall be great, and shall be called
    The Son of the Highest
    And the Lord God shall give unto him
    The throne of his father, David;
    And he shall reign over the House of Jacob

For ever;
And of his kingdom there shall be no end."

(*Mary wildly uncovers her eyes and looks up at the Angel.*)

1ST NARRATOR:

Then said Mary unto the angel,
"How shall this be,
Seeing I know not a man?"

2ND NARRATOR:

And the angel answered, and said unto her,
"The Holy Ghost shall come upon thee,
And the power of the Highest shall over-
    shadow thee;
Therefore also
That holy thing which shall be born of thee
Shall be called
The Son of God . . .
And, behold,
Thy cousin Elisabeth, she hath also conceived
    a son,
In her old age:
And this is the sixth month with her,
Who was called barren,
For with God nothing is impossible."

1ST NARRATOR:

And Mary said,

(*Mary spreads her arms wide open, and bows deeper.*)

"Behold, the handmaid of the Lord;
Be it unto me according to thy word."

(*The bright light fades from the archway. The Angel vanishes.*)

2ND NARRATOR:
> And the angel departed from her.

(*Pause*)

(*Mary rises from her knees. For a minute, as though not knowing what to do, she stands head bowed, face covered by her hands. She then turns, as though on an inspiration. She wraps the blue cloak she is wearing more closely round her. She stoops down to adjust the strap of a sandal.*)

2ND NARRATOR:
> And Mary arose, in those days,
> And went into the hill country
> With haste,
> Into the City of Judah.

1ST NARRATOR (*taking up*):
> Far from Nazareth . . .
> This was to be the first,
> And perhaps the strangest,
> And, to those who knew her, the most mysterious
> Of all Mary's journeys.
> Set out upon
> In haste,
> Solitary.
> Still hearing, forever hearing the Angel's saying.
> Those words go with her the winding roads,
> Through the steep, bare country,
> To the City of Judah,
> Where dwells Elisabeth.
> Elisabeth of the miracle,
> Mary's cousin.

(*Pause*)

To whom else can she turn
Now?
Set apart, to whom is Mary to speak
In her new need?
What other human being?
Aged Elisabeth, who has conceived,
Knows.
Nothing *is* impossible.
She in there,
She awaits the girl Mary,
She'll come to meet her.

(*While 1st Narrator speaks, Mary is moving towards the exit L. She halts to look back round the room, strangely, as though leaving all familiarity behind her. She stays where she is, for a minute more.*)

2ND NARRATOR:
Look upon Mary.
She has said,
"Be it unto me according to Thy Word."

Exit Mary, R. The STAGE, left empty, continues further to darken in silence till off-stage, in the distance, a voice begins to be heard singing the Magnificat.

During the singing—

Curtain

SOLO: Magnificat—by Soprano.

ACT III

The Shepherds

Symphony by Handel. Organ only.
Carol: "While Shepherds Watched Their Flocks by
Night."
SCENE: *A rocky field on a hillside.*
TIME: *Midnight, mid-winter.*
A ridge of rocks (above which the angels are to ap-
pear) runs across the background; other small rocks jut
out, here and there, in the foreground. In the shelter of
one of the rocks burns the shepherds' fire. The scene,
owing to the frosty starriness of the night, is not quite
dark. (N.B. This night scene, with its sere and primitive
harshness, should contrast in every possible way with the
night scene of Act I—the sombrely splendid lamp-glowing
interior of the King's tent.)
When the CURTAIN rises, the 1st Shepherd is on-
stage crouching over the fire, warming his hands. He is
heavily cloaked against the cold. His crook lies on the
ground beside him. Throughout the Narrators' words he
remains immobile, but once or twice he looks round him
awaiting his friends.

1ST NARRATOR:
    So still, so clear,
    So cold. . . .
    This midnight
    This is mid-winter
    The wind has dropped, but the rocks
    Seem haunted by it. . . .
    Over the hilly fields,
    Over the watching shepherds.

Over their flocks,
There is, now, silence—
Silence,
As though the Earth were holding her breath.

2ND NARRATOR:
Over the hills, yes,
Silence.
But the roads still are awake, awake in the dark.
There are still travellers,
Late-comers, stragglers.
Roads?
These are savage tracks, gutted by weather,
Stony under the foot
As the beds of torrents. . . .
Far off, far apart in the night,
Can be heard stumblings,
Shoutings,
The urging-along of mules or donkeys,
Or a voice singing or chanting,
To keep the courage up. . . .
And, strung out, here or there,
Go the jogging lanterns.

(*Pause*)

This is the country outside Bethlehem,
The City of David.
All today
—And for how many days before?—
There has been movement;
Men, women and children
Of the lineage of the House of David,
Streaming into Bethlehem,
To be numbered,
And then, taxed.

143

1ST NARRATOR:

    They are many. . . .
    How shall it contain them,
    This little city?
    Already,
    Bethlehem overflows.

    (*Pause*)

    They must do as they may,
    Fare as they can.
    This is a country under foreign rule,
    Living on the promise
    Of a Deliverer.
    Till He come,
    One obeys.
    Who dare ask questions
    When Rome has spoken?

2ND NARRATOR (*in a voice as though reading*):

    And it came to pass in those days,
    That there went out a decree
    From Caesar Augustus,
    That all the world should be taxed. . . .
    And all went to be taxed, every one into his
        own city.
    And Joseph also went up from Galilee,
    Out of the City of Nazareth, into Judaea,
    Unto the city of David,
    Which is called Bethlehem
    —Because he was of house and lineage
        of David—
    To be taxed,
    With Mary, his espoused wife,
    Being great with child.

1ST NARRATOR:
A harsh, cold, difficult journey . . .
For the anxious Joseph,
An anxious journey.
And then, when they got to Bethlehem
—Crowded Bethlehem—
What place for them?

2ND NARRATOR (*in a voice as though reading*):
And there were, in the same country,
Shepherds abiding in the field,
Keeping watch over their flock
By night.

(*1st Shepherd stirs to alert, hearing footsteps coming. He rises and signals by the light of the fire.*)

1ST SHEPHERD (*calling to off-stage*):
What kept you?
I lit the fire this long time.

Enter 2nd Shepherd.

2ND SHEPHERD:
Well, that you did:
I'm shrammed!

(*He goes close to the fire, lays down his crook and extends his hands.*)

One of them strayed.
I went after her up the gulley,
Then, not a sight of her.
I was out since dark,
Climbing the other side
By the cracks in the rocks.
She could have perished in one of those

145

—She's contrary. She's done that before on me;
There's no teaching her.
A fine height she'd got herself to
When I heard her crying.
And *then* I thought I'd be all night
Getting her down.

1ST SHEPHERD:
Well . . .
That's the way it is.

2ND SHEPHERD:
That's the way they are.
What gets into them?

1ST SHEPHERD:
There's no saying.

2ND SHEPHERD (*rubbing his chin, reflective*):
You'd need patience.

1ST SHEPHERD (*struck by a thought*):
Wouldn't you rather be an Emperor in Rome?

2ND SHEPHERD:
I would not.
Why would I?

1ST SHEPHERD:
Giving the orders?
Look at the way he has people running about—
Look at them now!

2ND SHEPHERD:
Has he sense, though?
What does *he* know?
He's not amongst us.
We know what *we* know,

146

But he doesn't know that. . . .
I shouldn't wonder he's an ignorant man.

1ST SHEPHERD:
Yet it could be a great thing to be a ruler?

2ND SHEPHERD:
An ignorant ruler could be a terrible thing.
This Emperor now, in Rome,
Could he care sheep?
Would he be faithful to them?
Would he know the country?
. . . You'd say, not?
Well, then,
Let him give out his orders!
He's free to.

(*Laughs*)

1ST SHEPHERD (slowly):
Should there be a faithful ruler,
I'd like to see him. . . .

2ND SHEPHERD (*mockingly*):
You and your great-grandson?

1ST SHEPHERD (*good-humouredly*):
Ah, be bothered to you!

Enter 3rd Shepherd. (His step has been quiet. The other two look up, startled.)

2ND SHEPHERD:
You came up quietly!

3RD SHEPHERD (*drawing nearer the fire*):
Like a thief—eh?
You are the two great watchmen,

147

You two!
Where are your ears?

1ST SHEPHERD:
We were gabbing, a bit.

3RD SHEPHERD:
I heard you.

(*Still standing, he leans on his crook, looks round.*)

It's a strange kind of night,
In its own way.
Did you see the light?

2ND SHEPHERD:
Lanterns, was it?
Along the Bethlehem road?

3RD SHEPHERD:
No.
I didn't say *lights,* I said *light.*
Away there—

(*gestures into the dark*)

Behind the hills,
In the sky. . . .

(*Pause*)

There *was* no singing—was there?

1ST SHEPHERD:
Was there?

3RD SHEPHERD (*impatient*):
I'm asking *you.*

2ND SHEPHERD:
Singing along the roads?

148

3RD SHEPHERD:
No.
I said, the *sky*
I didn't hear it, I didn't *yet* hear,
And yet,
Did I?

2ND SHEPHERD (*sarcastic*):
Only yourself can say.

3RD SHEPHERD (*unmoved*):
If I hadn't been awake,
I'd have thought I was dreaming.
No—no dream, though,
This was a great Wakening,
Wakening out of a dream.

(*Pause*)

I tell you,
My heart's as tight as a harp-string.

(*Pause*)

And what do you think I saw?
There's a new star.

(*The two others make no reply. He raises his voice.*)

I'm telling you,
There's a NEW STAR!

2ND SHEPHERD (*indulgent*):
Listen to the boy!

1ST SHEPHERD (*sleepy*):
Listen to the boy.

3RD SHEPHERD (*with violent, youthful impatience*):
A-a-a-ach!

*(He seats himself unwillingly, between his two com-
panions, crook across his knees, at the alert. Head turned,
he continues to watch the skyline, behind him. And the
skyline, as he watches, begins to brighten.)*

1ST NARRATOR:

Shepherds,
The sons of shepherds,
Who were the sons of shepherds,
Are weather-wise.
They know more than they say,
See more than they know,
Apprehend change.
Change in the weather of the soul,
Change in the weather of the world,
This night,
Christmas. . . .
Here are the three shepherds,
Our first witnesses.

2ND NARRATOR:

Abiding in the field,
Keeping watch over their flock
By night.

*(While 2nd Narrator is speaking, the sky over the
rockline fills up with radiance. In the heart of the radiance
appears the Angel.)*

1ST NARRATOR:

And, lo,
The angel of the Lord came upon them,
And the glory of the Lord shone round
about them

(shepherds show fear)

And they were sore afraid,
And the angel said unto them—

2ND NARRATOR:

"Fear not:
For, behold,
I bring you good tidings of great joy
Which shall be to all people.
For unto you is born, this day
In the city of David,
A Saviour, which is Christ the Lord.

(*Pause*)

And this shall be a sign unto you:
Ye shall find the babe
Wrapped in swaddling clothes,
Lying in a manger."

(*There are to appear, now, behind the Angel, ranks of Smaller Angels. These raise their arms when it comes to "Glory to God."*)

1ST NARRATOR:

And suddenly,
There was with the angel a multitude of the
    heavenly host,

(*Music: Choir and Organ*)

Praising God, and saying—
"Glory to God in the highest!
And on earth peace,
Good will toward men!"

(*The radiance fades out; the Angel and the Smaller Angels vanish from view.*)

2ND NARRATOR:

And it came to pass,
As the angels were gone away from them
    into heaven,

The shepherds said,
One to another—

(*The shepherds have turned to each other. They are eagerness, and yet all awe.*)

3RD SHEPHERD (*the first to collect himself*):
Let us now go.
Even unto Bethlehem!

2ND SHEPHERD:
And see this thing which is come to pass?

3RD SHEPHERD:
And see this thing which is come to pass?

1ST SHEPHERD:
Which the Lord hath made *known* unto us.

2ND SHEPHERD:
Made known unto *us*.

(*They pick their crooks up, gird themselves for the journey.*)

3RD SHEPHERD (*leading the way*):
Let us *now* go! Now!

(*The 1st and 2nd Shepherds eye one another, for a moment sharing the same trouble—that of good shepherds. ARE they to leave their flock? They look round them, away into the dark where their sheep are.*)

1ST SHEPHERD (*finally*):
May God guard them!

2ND SHEPHERD (*speaking up to the sky*):
Most High,
Look down on our sheep!
They are in Thy care.

152

Exit 3rd Shepherd. Exit 2nd and 1st Shepherd (one
with a hand on the other's shoulder).
STAGE remains empty.

1ST NARRATOR:
Their little fire
Will burn out
—No longer warming the rock—
Into white ash.
And then, gradually,
The new day,
Christmas,
Will brighten over the backs of the safe sheep,
Left here. . . .
The shepherds are in the streets,
Where the dawn gleams.
They are searching Bethlehem—
Not in vain.

Curtain

BEFORE ACT IV

Organ: *"Sheep May Safely Graze."*
Followed by *Carol: "The First Noël."*

ACT IV

The Adoration of the Shepherds

SCENE: *The stable in Bethlehem.*
TIME: *Christmas morning, early.*
The stable is in the form of a cave (as it would have been). Semi-dark, it recedes into darkness.
Such light as there is, which is tawny, is thrown upward by two or three lanterns placed on the floor. But also, light of a brighter and less earthly kind emanates from the crib. It shines on Mary's face, and (though less brightly) on the figure of Joseph.
The CURTAIN rises on Mary, seated behind the crib, looking down on it; on Joseph, standing behind her; on the half-seen form of the Babe in the crib.

1ST NARRATOR:
> In the lowly stable,
> The kindly stable
> —For there *was* no room for them in the inn—

2ND NARRATOR (*in voice as though reading*):
> She brought forth her first-born Son,

154

And wrapped him in swaddling clothes,
And laid him in a manger.

(*The three shepherds can be seen, beginning to
enter. They do so NOT directly on to the stage, by L. and
R. entrances, but APPROACHING the stage frontways,
down the aisle between onlookers.*)

1ST NARRATOR:

Here they come—see!
See, they have found their way!
Confused though they were
—Perhaps?—
By their own haste,
And confused by Bethlehem?
The city,
City of David, great in name—
In name—but
Only a name—till now?—
For those three countrymen.
Shepherds, whose world was their fields . . .
They have found their way.

(*The shepherds gather in a knot at the foot of the
centre steps leading up to the stage. They stand looking
upward into the stable. Then, one by one, they ascend the
steps.*)

2ND NARRATOR:

Last night,
A sky crowded with singing angels;
A sky dazzled—
All the glory of Heaven!
Now
They are drawing nigh to this quiet place,
Dusky, warmed by the breath

155

Of the tethered beasts . . .
They go between the lanterns, over the straw.

(Mary looks up from the crib and smiles at the shepherds. Joseph raises a hand in salutation. One by one, the shepherds approach the crib. Each stands looking down into it, then kneels.)

1ST NARRATOR:

They had carried lambs in their arms;
But never was there a more tender lamb
Than this Lamb of God,
New-born,

2ND NARRATOR:

"For unto you"
—The Angel had told them—
"For unto *you* is born, this day,
A Saviour,
Which is Christ the Lord."

(Pause)

He told them,
"I bring you glad tidings,
Of great joy."

1ST NARRATOR:

And joy fills the hearts
Of these first guests
Of the King of Kings.

(The shepherds rise from their knees, one by one. Each looks once more, for a moment, into the crib, bows low to Mary, salutes Joseph, then turns and comes down the centre steps, facing the onlookers. It can be seen from

the faces and bearing and gestures of the shepherds that they are filled with a joyous exaltation. They can hardly restrain themselves. At the foot of the steps, they again gather into a group, this time as though they were conferring. They go out—down the aisle between the onlookers—with eager haste. Hardly can they wait, now, to spread the news.)
    Exit the shepherds.

1ST NARRATOR:
    Out into the streets again,
    Go the shepherds,
    And *out* of the streets again,
    Into all the country—
    Great with what they have seen.

2ND NARRATOR *(voice as though reading)*:
    For, yes—
    When they had seen it,
    They made known abroad the saying which was
        told them
    Concerning this Child.
    And all they that heard it wondered at
        those things
    Which were told them by the shepherds.

    (Pause)

    And the shepherds returned,
    Glorifying and praising God.

    (While 2nd Narrator is speaking, Mary rises and, with Joseph's help, lifts the swaddled Babe from the crib. She stands holding the Babe against her breast, looking out over His head. She looks out as though into the distance. Once, she presses the Child more closely against her breast, as though to keep Him the more safe.)

157

1ST NARRATOR:
But Mary kept all these things,
And pondered them in her heart.

(*Pause*)

Curtain

Organ: "Largo"—Handel.
Carol: "As with Gladness Men of Old."

ACT V

The Adoration of the Magi

SCENE: *The stable.*
TIME: *Epiphany.*
At the beginning of this Act, the CURTAIN does
NOT *immediately rise. It is softly lit from in front. High*
up, over the top of the CURTAIN, hangs the star.

1ST NARRATOR:
> To the King of Kings,
> Journey the three Kings.

2ND NARRATOR (*voice as though reading*):
> Now when Jesus was born in Bethlehem
> Of Judaea,
> In the days of Herod the king,
> There came wise men from the East
> To Jerusalem,
> Saying—
> "Where is he that is born the King of the Jews?
> We have seen his Star in the East,
> And are come to worship Him."

1ST NARRATOR:
> In Jerusalem
> There is an earthly king,
> Who trembles.

2ND NARRATOR (*voice as though reading*):
> When Herod the king had heard these things,

He was troubled,
And all Jerusalem with him.
And,
When he had gathered all the chief priests
And scribes of the people together,
He demanded of them where Christ should
    be born.
And they said unto him—
"In Bethlehem of Judaea,
For thus it is written by the prophet."

(*Pause*)

Then Herod,
When he had privily called the wise men,
Inquired of them,
What time the star had appeared.
And
He sent them to Bethlehem and said—
"Go and search diligently for the young child;
And when ye have found him, bring me
    word again,
That I may come and worship him
Also."

1ST NARRATOR:
    To worship
    Was *not* King Herod's intent. . . .
    "He hath put down the mighty from their seats,"
    Mary had sung.

    (*Pause*)

    The Wise Men listened.

2ND NARRATOR (*voice as though reading*):
    When they had heard the king, they departed,
    And, lo,
    The star which they saw in the east

Went before them,

(*Organ music cue*)

Till

It came and stood over where the young
child was.

(*Introductory music to "Hallelujah" Chorus—Mount
of Olives Suite.*)

1ST NARRATOR:

The Star—
For which the alerted heavens,
Had waited;
For which these three watchers,
Far apart,
Each alone on his tower-top,
Had watched
—Risen!
The Sign, the guide,
It had led them. . . .
It comes to rest.

(*While 1st Narrator speaks the above words, the
three Kings begin to be seen advancing as did the shepherds, down the aisle between the onlookers.*)

2ND NARRATOR (*voice as though reading*):

When they saw the star,
They rejoiced with exceeding great joy.

(*Carol: "We Three Kings of Orient Are."*)

*While the 2nd Narrator is speaking, the CURTAIN
rises (or parts). We behold the stable is brilliantly lit, as
by sunny daylight (as though it had no roof but the
sky).*

*Mary (instead of leaning low over the crib) is en-
throned above it, her brilliantly blue cloak flowing down.
Flowers are strewn on the crib, on the hem of her cloak, on
the ground.*

161

Joseph stands not behind Mary (as he did before) but to the L. of the stage, forward, arms folded, looking towards the Child and Mary. He also seems to have taken on the dignity of an accepted destiny.

(From the minute before the CURTAIN rises, and while the three Kings ascend the steps, and onward through the action to follow, the carol "We Three Kings of Orient Are" is sung.)

The action and movements of each King—as, one after the other, they approach the crib, each raising his gift in the air, then placing it at the foot of the crib—must be slow, glorious and dramatic. This for them—it must be felt—is the culmination. In the nature of their humility must be felt their kingship. But also theirs is the kingdom of the mind. They are offering to the Child what they value most: the austerity of their wisdom, their wealth of learning.

1ST NARRATOR *(when the carol is done)*:

    The Child in the manger
    Has no crown;
    He lies not in purple or velvet
    But in sweet hay
    Smelling of summer.
    It is said,
    That when Mary laid her child there
    In the hay,
    The weeds in the scythed grasses
    Sprang into flower,
    For joy.
    The Child lay
    In a honey of vetch and clover,
    Kissed by wide-eyed daisies,
    And sky-blue borage.

2ND NARRATOR:

    And, see!
    —Kings are not the only comers!

NATIVITY PLAY

*Enter a Little Boy. (Some other children follow him,
more timidly. The boy stares for a moment at the Kings,
then goes on and makes his way to the crib.)*

BOY:

    How are you, Jesus?
    Look,
    We have come to see you!

    *(The other children also approach the crib, gathering
round.)*

    Are you as we are?
    Angels sang, they say
    —Is that true?

    (Pause)

    Your eyes are open,
    You see us, don't you?
    You love us, do you?
    I think you do.

    (Pause)

    You brought a Star with you;
    Because of You, Bethlehem has a Star.
    That shines night and day
    And *you* shine, Jesus,
    As though
    You were made of light.

    (Pause)

    When will you play?
    We have brought you treasures.

163

2ND NARRATOR:
O come, let us adore Him! *

"Adeste Fidelis" begins to be sung.

Trumpets

    * *Choir and organ:* 1st verse, lead singer.

CURTAIN

Notes on Writing
a Novel

PLOT—ESSENTIAL. The Pre-Essential.

Plot might seem to be a matter of choice. It is not. The particular plot is something the novelist is driven to. It is what is left after the whittling-away of alternatives. The novelist is confronted, at a moment (or at what appears to be the moment: actually its extension may be indefinite), by the impossibility of saying what is to be said in any other way.

He is forced towards his plot. By what? By the "what is to be said." What is "what is to be said"? A mass of subjective matter that has accumulated —impressions received, feelings about experience, distorted results of ordinary observation, and something else—*x*. This matter is *extra* matter. It is superfluous to the non-writing life of the writer. It is luggage left in the hall between two journeys, as opposed to the perpetual furniture of rooms. It is destined to be elsewhere. It cannot move till its destination is known. Plot is the knowing of destination.

Plot is diction. Action of language, language of action.

Plot is story. It is also "a story" in the nursery sense = lie. The novel lies, in saying that something happened that did not. It must, therefore, contain uncontradictable truth, to warrant the original lie.

Story involves action. Action towards an end not to be foreseen (by the reader) but also towards an end which, having *been* reached, must be seen to have been from the start inevitable.

Action by whom? The Characters (see CHAR-ACTERS). Action in view of what, and because of what? The "what is to be said."

What about the idea that the function of action is to *express* the characters? This is wrong. The characters are there to provide the action. Each character is created, and must only be so created, as to give his or her action (or, rather, contributory part in the novel's action) verisimilitude.

What about the idea that plot should be in-genious, complicated—a display of ingenuity re-markable enough to command attention? If more than such a display, what? Tension, or mystification towards tension, are good for emphasis. For their own sakes, bad.

Plot must further the novel towards its object. What object? The non-poetic statement of a poetic truth.

Have not all poetic truths been already stated?

The essence of a poetic truth is that no statement of it can be final.

Plot, story, is in itself un-poetic. At best it can only be not anti-poetic. It cannot claim a single poetic licence. It must be reasoned—onward from the moment when its none-otherness, its only-possibleness has become apparent. Novelist must always have one foot, sheer circumstantiality, to stand on, whatever the other foot may be doing. (N.B.— Much to be learnt from story-telling to children. Much to be learnt from the detective story—especially non-irrelevance. [See RELEVANCE.])

Flaubert's *"Il faut intéresser."* Stress on manner of telling: keep in mind, "I will a tale *unfold.*" Interest of watching silk handkerchief drawn from conjuror's watch.

Plot must not cease to move forward. (See ADVANCE.) The *actual* speed of the movement must be even. *Apparent* variations in speed are good, necessary, but there must be no actual variations in speed. To obtain those apparent variations is part of the illusion-task of the novel. Variations in texture can be made to give the effect of variations in speed. Why are *apparent* variations in speed necessary? (a) For emphasis. (b) For non-resistance, or "give," to the nervous time-variations of the reader. Why is *actual* evenness, non-variation, of speed necessary? For the sake of internal evenness for its own sake. Perfection of evenness =

perfection of control. The evenness of the speed should be the evenness inseparable from tautness. The tautness of the taut string is equal (or even) all along and at any part of the string's length.

CHARACTERS

Are the characters, then, to be constructed to formula—the formula pre-decided by the plot? Are they to be drawn, cut out, jointed, wired, in order to be manipulated for the plot?

No. There is no question as to whether this would be right or wrong. It would be impossible. One cannot "make" characters, only marionettes. The manipulated movement of the marionette is not the "action" necessary for plot. Characterless action is not action at all, in the plot sense. It is the indivisibility of the act from the actor, and the inevitability of *that* act on the part of *that* actor, that gives action verisimilitude. Without that, action is without force or reason. Forceless, reasonless action disrupts plot. The term "creation of character" (or characters) is misleading. Characters pre-exist. They are *found*. They reveal themselves slowly to the novelist's perception—as might fellow-travellers seated opposite one in a very dimly-lit railway carriage.

The novelist's perceptions of his characters take place *in the course of the actual writing of the novel*. To an extent, the novelist is in the same position as his reader. But his perceptions should be always just in advance.

The ideal way of presenting character is to invite perception.

In what do the characters pre-exist? I should say, in the mass of matter (see PLOT) that had accumulated before the inception of the novel.

(N.B.—The unanswerability of the question, from an outsider: "Are the characters in your novel invented, or are they from real life?" Obviously, neither is true. The outsider's notion of "real life" and the novelist's are hopelessly apart.)

How, then, is the pre-existing character—with its own inner spring of action, its contrarieties—to be made to play a pre-assigned role? In relation to character, or characters, once these have been contemplated, *plot* must at once seem over-rigid, arbitrary.

What about the statement (in relation to PLOT) that "each character is created in order, and only in order, that he or she may supply the required action?" To begin with, strike out "created." Better, the character is *recognised* (by the novelist) by the signs he or she gives of unique capacity to act in a certain way, which "certain way" fulfils a need of the plot.

The character is there (in the novel) for the sake of the action he or she is to contribute to the plot. Yes. But also, he or she exists *outside* the action being contributed to the plot.

Without that existence of the character outside the (necessarily limited) action, the action itself would be invalid.

Action is the simplification (for story purposes) of complexity. For each one act, there are an x number of rejected alternatives. It is the palpable presence of the alternatives that gives action interest. Therefore, in each of the characters, while he or she is acting, the play and pull of alternatives must be felt. It is in being seen to be capable of alternatives that the character becomes, for the reader, valid.

Roughly, the action of a character should be unpredictable before it has been shown, inevitable when it has been shown. In the first half of a novel, the unpredictability should be the more striking. In the second half, the inevitability should be the more striking.

(Most exceptions to this are, however, masterpiece-novels. In *War and Peace, L'Éducation sentimentale* and *À la Recherche du temps perdu,* unpredictability dominates up to the end.)

The character's prominence in the novel (pre-decided by the plot) decides the character's range —of alternatives. The novelist must allot (to the point of rationing) psychological space. The "hero," "heroine" and "villain" (if any) are, by agreement, allowed most range. They are entitled, for the portrayal of their alternatives, to time and space. Placing the characters in receding order to their importance to the plot, the number of their alternatives may be seen to diminish. What E. M. Forster has called the "flat" character has no alternatives at all.

The ideal novel is without "flat" characters.

Characters must *materialise*—i.e., must have a palpable physical reality. They must be not only see-able (visualisable); they must be to be felt. Power to give physical reality is probably a matter of the extent and nature of the novelist's physical sensibility, or susceptibility. In the main, English novelists are weak in this, as compared to French and Russians. Why?

Hopelessness of categoric "description." Why? Because this is static. Physical personality belongs to action: cannot be separated from it. Pictures must be in movement. Eyes, hands, stature, etc., must appear, and only appear, *in play*. Reaction to physical personality is part of action—love, or sexual passages, only more marked application of this general rule.

(Conrad an example of strong, non-sexual use of physical personality.)

The materialisation (in the above sense) of the character for the novelist must be instantaneous. It happens. No effort of will—and obviously no effort of intellect—can induce it. The novelist can *use* a character that has not yet materialised. But the unmaterialised character represents an enemy pocket in an area that has been otherwise cleared.

This cannot go on for long. It produces a halt in plot.

When the materialisation *has* happened, the chapters written before it happened will almost certainly have to be recast. From the plot point of view, they will be found invalid.

Also, it is essential that for the reader the materialisation of the character should begin early. I say begin, because for the *reader* it may, without harm, be gradual.

Is it from this failure, or tendency to fail, in materialisation that the English novelist depends so much on engaging emotional sympathy for his characters?

Ruling sympathy out, a novel must contain at least one *magnetic* character. At least one character capable of keying the reader up, as though he (the reader) were in the presence of someone he is in love with. This is not a rule of salesmanship but a pre-essential of *interest*. The character must do to the reader what he has done to the novelist—magnetise towards himself perceptions, sense-impressions, desires.

The unfortunate case is, where the character has, obviously, acted magnetically upon the author, but fails to do so upon the reader.

There must be combustion. Plot depends for its movement on internal combustion.

Physically, characters are almost always copies, or composite copies. Traits, gestures, etc., are searched for in, and assembled from, the novelist's memory. Or a picture, a photograph or the cinema screen may be drawn on. Nothing physical can be *invented*. (Invested physique stigmatises the inferior novel.) Proust (in last volume) speaks of this assemblage of traits. Though much may be lifted from a specific person in "real life," no person in "real life" could supply everything (physical) necessary for the character in the novel. No such person could have just that exact degree of physical intensity required for the character.

Greatness of characters is the measure of the unconscious greatness of the novelist's vision. They are "true" in so far as he is occupied with poetic truth. Their degrees in realness show the degrees of his concentration.

SCENE—Is a derivative of Plot.
Gives actuality to Plot.

Nothing can happen nowhere. The locale of the happening always colours the happening, and often, to a degree, shapes it.

Plot having pre-decided what is to happen, scene, scenes, must be so found, so chosen, as to give the happening the desired force.

Scene, being physical, is, like the physical traits of the characters, generally a copy, or a composite copy. It, too, is assembled—out of memories which, in the first place, may have had no rational connection with one another. Again, pictures, photographs, the screen are sources of supply. Also dreams.

Almost anything drawn from "real life"—house, town, room, park, landscape—will almost certainly be found to require *some* distortion for the purposes of the plot. Remote memories, already distorted by the imagination, are most useful for the purposes of scene. Unfamiliar or once-seen places yield more than do familiar, often-seen places.

Wholly invented scene is as unsatisfactory (thin) as wholly invented physique for a character.

Scene, much more than character, is inside the novelist's conscious power. More than any other constituent of the novel, it makes him conscious *of* his power.

This can be dangerous. The weak novelist is always, compensatorily, scene-minded. (Jane Austen's economy of scene-painting, and her abstentions from it in what might be expected contexts, could in itself be proof of her mastery of the novel.)

Scene is only justified in the novel where it can be shown, or at least felt, to act upon action or character. In fact, where it has dramatic use.

Where not intended for dramatic use, scene is a sheer slower-down. Its staticness is a dead weight. It cannot make part of the plot's movement by being shown *in play*. (Thunderstorms, the sea, landscape flying past car or railway-carriage windows are not scene but *happenings*.)

The deadeningness of straight and prolonged "description" is as apparent with regard to scene as it is with regard to character. Scene must be evoked. For its details relevance (see RELEVANCE) is essential. Scene must, like the characters, not fail to materialise. In this it follows the same law—instantaneous for the novelist, gradual for the reader.

In "setting a scene" the novelist directs, or attempts to direct, the reader's visual imagination. He must allow for the fact that the reader's memories will not correspond with his own. Or, at least, not at all far along the way.

DIALOGUE—Must (1) *Further Plot.*
(2) *Express Character.*

Should not on any account be a vehicle for ideas for their own sake. Ideas only permissible where they provide a key to the character who expresses them.

Dialogue requires more art than does any other constituent of the novel. Art in the *celare artem* sense. Art in the trickery, self-justifying distortion sense. Why? Because dialogue must appear realistic without being so. Actual realism—the lifting, as it were, of passages from a stenographer's take-down of a "real life" conversation—would be disruptive. Of what? Of the illusion of the novel. In "real life" everything is diluted; in the novel everything is condensed.

What are the realistic qualities to be imitated (or faked) in novel dialogue? Spontaneity. Artless or hit-or-miss arrival at words used. Ambiguity (speaker not sure, himself, what he means). Effect of choking (as in engine): more to be said that can come through. Irrelevance. Allusiveness. Erraticness: unpredictable course. Repercussion.

What must novel dialogue, behind mask of these faked realistic qualities, really be and do? It must be pointed, intentional, relevant. It must crystallise situation. It must express character. It must advance plot.

During dialogue, the characters confront one another. The confrontation is in itself an occasion. Each one of these occasions, throughout the novel, is unique. Since the last confrontation, something has changed, advanced. What is being said is the effect of something that has happened; at the same time, what is being said *is in itself something happening,* which will, in turn, leave its effect.

Dialogue is the ideal means of showing what is between the characters. It crystallises relationships. It *should,* ideally, so be effective as to make analysis or explanation of the relationships between the characters unnecessary.

Short of a small range of physical acts—a fight, murder, love-making—dialogue is the most vigorous and visible inter-action of which characters in a novel are capable. Speech is what the characters *do to each other*.

Dialogue provides means for the psychological materialisation of the characters. It should short-circuit description of mental traits. Every sentence in dialogue should be descriptive of the character who is speaking. Idiom, tempo and shape of each spoken sentence should be calculated by novelist, towards this descriptive end.

Dialogue is the first case of the novelist's need for notation from real life. Remarks or turns of phrase indicatory of class, age, degree of intellectual pretension, *idées reçues,* nature and strength of governing fantasy, sexual temperament, persecution-sense or acumen (fortuitous arrival at general or poetic truth) should be collected. (N.B.— Proust, example of this semi-conscious notation and putting to use of it.)

All the above, from *class* to *acumen,* may already have been established, with regard to each character, by a direct statement by the novelist to the reader. It is still, however, the business of dialogue to show these factors, or qualities, in play.

There must be present in dialogue—i.e., in each sentence spoken by each character—*either* (a) calculation, or (b) involuntary self-revelation.

Each piece of dialogue *must* be "something happening." Dialogue *may* justify its presence by being "illustrative"—but this secondary use of it must be watched closely, challenged. Illustrative-ness can be stretched too far. Like straight description, it then becomes static, a dead weight—halting the movement of the plot. The "amusing" for its *own* sake should above all be censored. So should infatuation with any idiom.

The functional use of dialogue for the plot must be the first thing in the novelist's mind. Where functional usefulness cannot be established, dialogue must be left out.

What is this functional use? That of a bridge.

Dialogue is the thin bridge which must, from time to time, carry the entire weight of the novel. Two things to be kept in mind—(a) the bridge is there to permit *advance,* (b) the bridge must be strong enough for the weight.

Failure in any one piece of dialogue is a loss, at once to the continuity and the comprehensibility of the novel.

Characters should, on the whole, be under rather than over articulate. What they *intend* to say should be more evident, more striking (because of its greater inner importance to the plot) than what they arrive at *saying.*

ANGLE

The question of *angle* comes up twice over in the novel. Angle has two senses—(a) visual, (b) moral.

(a) *Visual Angle.*—This has been much

discussed—particularly I think by Henry James. Where is the camera-eye to be located? (1) In the breast or brow of *one* of the characters? This is, of course, simplifying and integrating. But it imposes on the novel the limitations of the "I"—whether the first person is explicitly used or not. Also, with regard to any matter that the specific character does not (cannot) know, it involves the novelist in long cumbrous passages of cogitation, speculation and guesses. E.g., of any character other than the specific (or virtual) "I," it must always be "he appeared to feel," "he could be seen to see," rather than "he felt," "he saw." (2) In the breast or brow of a succession of characters? This is better. It *must,* if used, involve very careful, considered division of the characters, by the novelist, in the *seeing* and the *seen.* Certain characters gain in importance and magnetism by being only *seen:* this makes them more romantic, fatal-seeming, sinister. In fact, no character in which these qualities are, for the plot, essential should be allowed to enter the *seeing* class. (3) In the breast or brow of omniscient story-teller (the novelist)? This, though appearing naïve, would appear best. The novelist should retain right of entry, at will, into any of the characters: their memories, sensations and thought-processes should remain his, to requisition for appropriate use. What conditions "appropriateness"? The demands of the plot. Even so, the novelist must not lose sight of point made above—the gain in necessary effect, for some characters, of their remaining *seen*—their remaining closed, apparently, even to the omniscience of the novelist.

The cinema, with its actual camera-work, is interesting study for the novelist. In a good film, the camera's movement, angle and distance have all worked towards one thing—the fullest possible realisation of the director's idea, the completest possible surrounding of the subject. Any trick is justified if it adds a statement. With both film and novel, plot is the pre-imperative. The novelist's relation to the novel is that of the director's relation to the film. The cinema, cinema-going, has no doubt built up in novelists a great authoritarianism. This seems to me good.

(b) *Moral Angle.*—This too often means, pre-assumptions—social, political, sexual, national, aesthetic, and so on. These may all exist, sunk at different depths, in the same novelist. Their existence cannot fail to be palpable; and their nature determines, more than anything else, the sympatheticness or antipatheticness of a given novel to a given circle of readers.

Pre-assumptions are bad. They limit the novel to a given circle of readers. They cause the novel to act immorally *on* that given circle. (The lady asking the librarian for a "nice" novel to take home is, virtually, asking for a novel whose pre-assumptions will be identical with her own.) Outside the given circle, a novel's pre-assumptions must invalidate it for all other readers. The increasingly bad smell of most pre-assumptions probably accounts for the growing prestige of the detective story: the detective story works on the single, and universally acceptable, pre-assumption that an act of violence is anti-social, and that the doer, in the name of injured society, must be traced.

Great novelists write without pre-assumption. They write from outside their own nationality, class or sex.

To write thus should be the ambition of any novelist who wishes to state poetic truth.

Does this mean he must have no angle, no moral viewpoint? No, surely. Without these, he would be (a) incapable of maintaining the *conviction* necessary for the novel; (b) incapable of *lighting* the characters, who to be seen at all must necessarily be seen in a moral light.

From what source, then, must the conviction come? And from *what* morality is to come the light to be cast on the characters?

The conviction must come from certainty of the validity of the truth the novel is to present. The "moral light" has not, actually, a moral source; it is moral (morally powerful) according to the strength of its power of revelation. Revelation of what? The virtuousness or non-virtuousness of the action of the character. What is virtue in action?

185

Truth in action. Truth by what ruling, in relation
to what? Truth by the ruling of, and in relation to,
the inherent poetic truth that the novel states.

The presence, and action, of the poetic truth
is the motive (or motor) morality of the novel.

The direction of the action of the poetic truth
provides—in fact, *is*—the moral angle of the novel.
If he remains with that truth in view, the novelist
has no option as to his angle.

The action, or continuous line of action, of a
character is "bad" in so far as it runs counter to,
resists or attempts to deny, the action of the poetic
truth. It is predisposition towards such action that
constitutes "badness" in a character.

"Good" action, or "goodness" in the character,
from predisposition towards such action, is movement along with, expressive of and contributory to,
the action of the poetic truth.

If the novelist's moral angle is (a) decided by
recognition of the poetic truth, and (b) maintained
by the necessity of stating the truth by showing the
truth's action, it will be, as it should be, impersonal.
It will be, and (from the "interest" point of view)
will be able to stand being, pure of pre-assumptions
—national, social, sexual, etc.

(N.B.—"Humour" is the weak point in the
front against pre-assumptions. Almost all English
humour shows social [sometimes, now, backed by
political] pre-assumptions. [Extreme cases—that
the lower, or employed, classes are quaint or funny

—that aristocrats, served by butlers, are absurd. National pre-assumptions show in treatment of foreigners.])

ADVANCE

It has been said that plot must advance; that the underlying (or inner) speed of the advance must be even. How is this arrived at?

1. Obviously, first, by the succession, the succeedingness, of events or happenings. It is to be remembered that *everything* put on record at all— an image, a word spoken, an interior movement of thought or feeling on the part of a character—is an event or happening. These proceed out of one another, give birth to one another, in a continuity that must be (a) obvious, (b) unbroken.

2. Every happening cannot be described, stated. The reader must be made to feel that what has not been described or stated has, nonetheless, happened. How? By the showing of subsequent events or happenings whose source *could* only have been in what has not actually been stated. Tuesday is Tuesday by virtue of being the day following Monday. The stated Tuesday must be shown as a derivative of the unstated Monday.

3. For the sake of emphasis, time must be falsified. But the novelist's consciousness of the subjective, arbitrary and emotional nature of the falsification should be evident to the reader. Against

this falsification—in fact, increasing the force of its effect by contrast—a clock should be heard always impassively ticking away at the same speed. The passage of time, and its demarcation, should be a factor in plot. The either concentration or even or uneven spacing-out of events along time is important.

The statement "Ten years had passed," or the statement "It was now the next day"—each of these is an event.

4. Characters most of all promote, by showing, the advance of the plot. How? By the advances, from act to act, in their action. By their showing (by emotional or physical changes) the effects both of action and of the passage of time. The diminution of the character's alternatives shows (because it is the work of) advance—by the end of a novel the character's alternatives, many at the beginning, have been reduced to almost none. In the novel, everything that happens happens either *to* or *because* of one of the characters. By the end of the novel, the character has, like the silkworm at work on the cocoon, spun itself out. Completed action is marked by the exhaustion (from one point of view) of the character. Throughout the novel, each character is expending potentiality. This expense of potentiality must be felt.

5. Scene promotes, or contributes to, advance by its freshness. Generically, it is fresh, striking, from being unlike the scene before. It is the new

"here and now." Once a scene ceases to offer freshness, it is a point-blank enemy to advance. Frequent change of scene *not* being an imperative of the novel—in fact, many novels by choice, and by wise choice, limiting themselves severely in this matter—how is there to continue to be freshness? By means of ever-differing presentation. Differing because of what? Season of year, time of day, effects of a happening (e.g., with house, rise or fall in family fortunes, an arrival, a departure, a death), beholding character's mood. At the first presentation, the *scene* has freshness; afterwards, the freshness must be in the *presentation*. The same scene can, by means of a series of presentations, each having freshness, be made to ripen, mature, to actually advance. The *static* properties in scene can be good for advance when so stressed as to show advance by contrast—advance on the part of the characters. Striking "unchangingness" gives useful emphasis to change. Change should not be a factor, at once, in *both* scene and character; either unchanged character should see, or be seen against, changed scene, or changed character should see, or be seen against, unchanged scene. *Two* changes obviously cancel each other out, and would cancel each other's contribution to the advance of plot.

RELEVANCE

Relevance—the question of it—is the headache of novel-writing.

189

As has been said, the model for relevance is the well-constructed detective story: nothing is "in" that does not tell. But the detective story is, or would appear to be, simplified by having *fact* as its kernel. The detective story makes towards concrete truth; the novel makes towards abstract truth.

With the detective story, the question "relevant to *what?*" can be answered by the intelligence. With the novel, the same question must constantly, and in every context, be referred to the intuition. The intelligence, in a subsequent check-over, may detect, but cannot itself put right, blunders, lapses or false starts on the part of the intuition.

In the notes on Plot, Character, Scene and Dialogue, everything has come to turn, by the end, on relevance. It is seen that all other relevances are subsidiary to the relevance of the plot—i.e., the relevance to itself that the plot demands. It is as contributory, in fact relevant, to plot that character, scene and dialogue are examined. To be perfectly contributory, these three must be perfectly relevant. If character, scene or dialogue has been weakened by anything irrelevant *to itself,* it can only be imperfectly relevant—which must mean, to a degree disruptive—to the plot.

The main hope for character (for each character) is that it should be magnetic—i.e., that it should *attract* its parts. This living propensity of the character to assemble itself, to integrate itself, to make itself in order to *be* itself will not, obviously, be resisted by the novelist. The magnetic, or magnetising, character can be trusted as to what is relevant *to itself*. The trouble comes when what is relevant to the character is found to be not relevant to the plot. At this point, the novelist must adjudicate. It is possible that the character may be right; it is possible that there may be some flaw in the novelist's sense of what is relevant to the plot.

Again, the character may, in fact must, decide one half of the question of relevance in dialogue. The character attracts to itself the right, in fact the only possible, idiom, tempo and phraseology for *that* particular character in speech. In so far as dialogue is *illustrative,* the character's, or characters', pull on it must not be resisted.

But in so far as dialogue must be "something happening"—part of action, a means of advancing plot—the other half of the question of dialogue-relevance comes up. Here, the pull from the characters may conflict with the pull from the plot. Here again the novelist must adjudicate. The recasting and recasting of dialogue that is so often necessary is, probably, the search for ideal compromise.

Relevance in scene is more straightforward. Chiefly, the novelist must control his infatuation with his own visual power. *No* non-contributory image, must be the rule. Contributory to what? To the mood of the "now," the mood that either projects or reflects action. It is a good main rule that objects—chairs, trees, glasses, mountains, cushions

—introduced into the novel should be stage-properties, necessary for "business." It will be also recalled that the well-set stage shows many objects *not* actually necessary for "business," but that these have a right to place by being descriptive—explanatory. In a play, the absence of the narrating voice makes it necessary to establish the class, period and general psychology of the characters by means of objects that can be seen. In the novel, such putting of objects to a descriptive (explanatory) use is excellent—alternative to the narrator's voice.

In scene, then, relevance demands either usefulness for action or else explanatory power in what is shown. There is no doubt that with some writers (Balzac, sometimes Arnold Bennett) categoricalness, in the presentation of scene, is effective. The aim is, usually, to suggest, by multiplication and exactitude of detail, either a scene's material oppressiveness or its intrinsic authority. But in general, for the purposes of most novelists, the number of objects genuinely necessary for explanation will be found to be very small.

Irrelevance, in any part, is a cloud and a drag on, a weakener of, the novel. It dilutes meaning. Relevance crystallises meaning.

The novelist's—any writer's—object is to whittle down his meaning to the exactest and finest possible point. What, of course, is fatal is when he does not know what he does mean: he has no point to sharpen.

Much irrelevance is introduced into novels by the writer's vague hope that at least some of this *may* turn out to be relevant, after all. A good deal of what might be called provisional writing goes to the first drafts of first chapters of most novels. At a point in the novel's progress, relevance becomes clearer. The provisional chapters are then recast.

The most striking fault in work by young or beginning novelists, submitted for criticism, is irrelevance—due either to infatuation or indecision. To direct such an author's attention to the imperative of relevance is certainly the most useful—and possibly the only—help that can be given.

A Note About the Author

Born in 1899 in Ireland, Elizabeth Bowen was uprooted early in her life and taken to England, where she received her schooling. In her twenties she discovered the delights of travel, and her first novel, *The Hotel,* grew out of one of her early sojourns in Italy. After the publication of her first short stories in 1923, Elizabeth Bowen published six collections of short stories and nine novels, among them *To the North* (1933), *The House in Paris* (1936), *The Death of the Heart* (1939), *The Heat of the Day* (1949), *A World of Love* (1955), *The Little Girls* (1964), and *Eva Trout* (1968). Her non-fiction books were made up of essays, travel writings, and recollections. After her marriage to Alan Cameron, she lived in Old Headington, Oxford, and returned there for a spell again after finally leaving her family home, Bowen's Court, in County Cork. But the latter part of her life in England was spent at Hythe, Kent, where she was when she died in 1973.

A NOTE ON THE TYPE

The text of this book was set on the Linotype in a face called TIMES ROMAN, designed by STANLEY MORISON for *The Times* (London), and first introduced by that newspaper in 1932.

Among typographers and designers of the twentieth century, Stanley Morison has been a strong forming influence, as typographical adviser to the English Monotype Corporation, as a director of two distinguished English publishing houses, and as a writer of sensibility, erudition, and keen practical sense.

In 1930 Morison wrote: "Type design moves at the pace of the most conservative reader. The good type-designer therefore realises that, for a new fount to be successful, it has to be so good that only very few recognise its novelty. If readers do not notice the consummate reticence and rare discipline of a new type, it is probably a good letter." It is now generally recognized that in the creation of *Times Roman* Morison successfully met the qualifications of this theoretical doctrine.

Composed, printed, and bound by Kingsport Press, Inc., Kingsport, Tennessee. Typography and binding design by

WARREN  CHAPPELL